/—
W

D0752201

PLAN YOUR HOME WITH
FENG SHUI

PLAN YOUR HOME WITH
FENG SHUI

IAN BRUCE

quantum

LONDON • NEW YORK • TORONTO • SYDNEY

quantum

An imprint of W. Foulsham & Co. Ltd
The Publishing House, Bennetts Close,
Cippenham, Slough, Berkshire SL1 5AP, England

ISBN 0-572-02395-2

The author and publisher would like to thank
the people who allowed their homes to be
photographed for this book.

Photographs by Paul Silverberg
Illustrations by Paul Colsell
Typeset in Great Britain by Grafica, Bournemouth
Printed in Great Britain

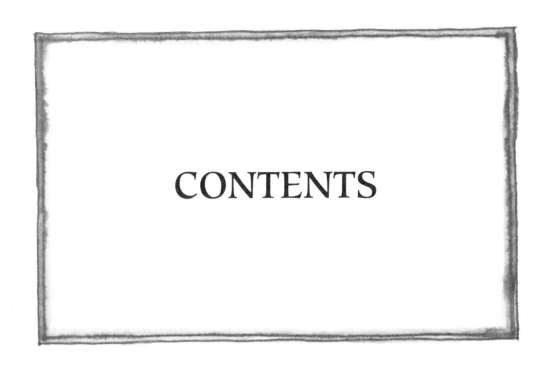

CONTENTS

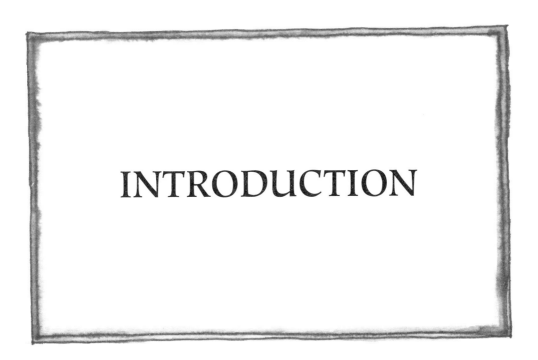

INTRODUCTION

What leads so many people to set aside today's complex technologies and focus instead on the simple practices of a metaphysical art which is older than Christianity? Why is Feng Shui as popular today in the Western world as it has been in the East for many centuries?

The only possible explanation, and one to which many thousands of people will testify, is that Feng Shui gets results. Whether your objective is to improve your love life, career or financial status, or simply to experience a greater level of tranquillity in your life, Feng Shui can make it happen. All you need is a basic understanding of the art and know how to implement it.

This book aims to provide you with that understanding and knowledge as effectively as possible. It is written in a practical, down-to-earth style to provide you with an extremely accessible 'hands-on' manual, which explains, step by step, exactly what you should do to make each room in your home comply with the beneficial laws of Feng Shui.

The benefits of Feng Shui are enormous. It can help you improve any and every area of your life painlessly, simply and effectively. For example, this book will reveal:

✳ How changing the position of your bed can revolutionise your sex life;

✳ How you can gain more wealth and material prosperity;

✳ How you can dramatically improve your chances of success in business or academic study, or find a new career which is both lucrative and enjoyable;

✳ How you can create an environment which helps everyone within your home communicate clearly and enjoy better personal relationships;

✳ How the principles of Feng Shui can be used to increase the physical, spiritual and emotional health of you and your family.

After introducing you to the general philosophies of Feng Shui, I discuss the key principles which can be applied throughout your home. This will give you a solid base of practical knowledge which you may then use as you wish.

Each part of your home – lounge, kitchen, dining room, bedrooms etc. – is then tackled chapter by chapter. This allows us to delve into the specifics of Feng Shui in a wide variety of situations and discuss how the principles can be used to create a more balanced environment which can attract more health, wealth, energy and tranquillity into your life.

Finally, we will take a look at how all this fits together to create an ideal Feng Shui home, and what benefits you can expect from following the principles you have learned.

To get the best out of *Plan your Home with Feng Shui*, I suggest you use the book in the following way:

✳ Read through the entire book from beginning to end, much as you would a novel. This will give you an overview of the subject and a good idea of the steps you will need to take to transform your home and life.

✳ Refer to the relevant chapters of the book as you begin putting the principles into action. For example, when you start tackling a bedroom, refer to Chapter 6 and use it as a practical guide. Remember, reading a book of recipes will not automatically provide you with a delicious meal; you must act on what you read. The same applies to this book. If you want to use Feng Shui to improve your life, you must spend some time putting the principles into action.

✳ Use the Improve Your Lifestyle section at the end of Chapters 3–9 for advice on how Feng Shui can help you cope with common problems.

So, welcome to *Plan your Home with Feng Shui!* Let the application of the principles in this book help you reach the highest levels of health, wealth and happiness.

Ian Bruce

1

THE PHILOSOPHY
The Art of
Feng Shui

Most people know that Feng Shui has its origins in the East, but contrary to popular opinion, Feng Shui is not an Eastern religion. It is more of an art: a way of harnessing the power of several metaphysical philosophies and combining them scientifically to bring about very real changes. These changes can include the attraction of wealth, increases in physical and emotional health and the cultivation of an overall sense of tranquillity and well-being.

Feng Shui literally means 'wind water' and – as you will see later – this reflects the fact that the primary aim of this ancient art is to restore a balanced flow of energy to your life and environment. It is thought by many that Feng Shui originated in China about 4,000 years before the birth of Christ, but no actual date can be given with any real sense of confidence. All we do know with certainty is that the art is older than Christianity and has gained a massive following in the West over the last few decades.

Just as a cake is made up of several different ingredients, all of which are vital to the whole, so Feng Shui is a system which can be reduced to several major philosophies and beliefs. So you gain a good understanding of how Feng Shui works, let's now consider these different elements in turn. Bear in mind, however, that each element is as important as the next, and so no 'order of importance' can be assumed.

CH'I

Ch'i (meaning 'breath') is the name given to a subtle electro-magnetic energy which flows through the entirety of the physical universe and within each individual human being. It is, in essence, a spiritual energy which has a great influence over our lives. That influence can either be positive or negative, depending on how well (or how badly) the Ch'i flows through ourselves and the environment.

Bodily Ch'i

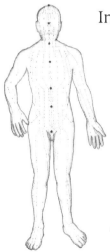

In the body of an individual, Ch'i flows in much the same way as blood, along meridians, which can be likened to arteries. There are 14 major meridians along which the Ch'i travels to and from major energy centres called chakras. There are seven chakras in all, and they are positioned as follows:

Working vertically down from the top of the body, the chakras are called:
Crown Chakra – at the crown of the head
Third-eye Chakra – between the eyebrows

Throat Chakra – at the throat
Heart Chakra – at the heart
Plexus Chakra – at the solar plexus
Navel Chakra – at the navel
Groin Chakra – at the groin.

We have likened the flow of Ch'i to that of blood, but Ch'i is not restricted by the physical boundaries of the body. Instead it extends as an aura, creating a kind of 'Ch'i bubble' which envelops the body. Like fingerprints, this aura is unique to each individual and its state is affected by various factors such as emotion, health and environment.

The size of the aura is typically dictated by the personality of the individual. People who are shy and reserved will tend to have an aura which extends just a few centimetres from their physical body. People who are more extrovert and good at communicating with others will tend to have an aura which extends perhaps 30 centimetres or even more from the physical boundary.

Consider public speakers who have the ability to arouse the emotions of their audience. Some might say this ability is exclusively the result of public-speaking skills. Feng Shui practitioners, on the other hand, would tell you that a good speaker has an extensive aura which causes everyone nearby to react emotionally.

This is because the auras which surround us merge when in close proximity with others, automatically exchanging emotional vibrations without us being consciously aware of it. This is why, on occasion, we find ourselves extremely uncomfortable in the presence of a particular individual, even when no words have been spoken. It also explains why we find that some people have almost 'magnetic personalities', which we are inexplicably drawn towards.

In a perfectly healthy human being the Ch'i energy flows freely throughout the body, but in times of stress or illness the Ch'i will be out of balance, and this must be corrected if the situation is to improve. By stimulating the chakras through meditation and visualisation exercises, any blockages in the Ch'i flow can be removed and normal emotional health will be regained.

It is no good enhancing the Ch'i of an environment if your bodily Ch'i is flowing badly, because the benefits will be negligible. The best way to ensure that you get the most out of Feng Shui is to begin enhancing the flow of your bodily Ch'i by meditating for 15 minutes or so a day. There are a number of methods of meditation which can be of help, but to begin with try using one of the two methods presented below:

Watch the breaths

Sit in a comfortable position and make sure that your back is as straight as possible. Close your eyes and relax completely. When your body feels comfortable and relaxed, focus your concentration on the nostrils. Watch the breaths. Do not count your breaths, but simply watch the air flow in and out of your nostrils with as much detachment as possible. If your mind wanders do not worry. Simply bring your attention back to watching the breaths.

You will find that as you do this your rate of breathing slows and your mind becomes very clear. As you practise this exercise on a daily basis your bodily Ch'i will regain a good sense of balance and you will notice that your emotions also become more stable, resulting in an inner sense of peace and harmony which is difficult to describe but easy to experience.

Chakra meditation

Once again sit in a comfortable position with your back as straight as possible. Relax your body completely and then focus on each of the seven chakras in turn. Begin with the groin chakra and imagine a swirling catherine wheel of energy at your groin. Concentrate on this image for a few minutes and then progress to the navel chakra, heart chakra and so on, culminating with the crown chakra.

This meditation stimulates the chakras and enhances bodily Ch'i flow. Many people find that when they do this exercise they experience tingling sensations or a sense of light-headedness. This is perfectly normal and indicates that the chakras are indeed being stimulated properly.

Environmental Ch'i

As well as flowing within the physical body of an individual, Ch'i also flows through the environment and external universe. The flow of Ch'i through the environment can also be either smooth or more obstructed, and this will naturally contribute towards positive or negative life experiences. In a perfectly natural environment, Ch'i flows with amazing freedom, creating an atmosphere of balance and harmony.

In more artificial environments the Ch'i is often obstructed by furniture or man-made structures and this creates an atmosphere which is more chaotic and awkward. This disruption of Ch'i is illustrated below:

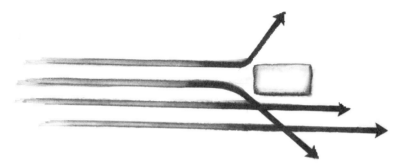

Although Ch'i cannot be seen, its effects are readily felt on an instinctive level. Compare the tranquil feeling of walking along a beach with the more stressful sensations associated with fighting your way through rush-hour traffic in a large town or city, and this becomes readily apparent. On the beach the environmental Ch'i flows smoothly, encouraging your bodily Ch'i to become more balanced and thus your emotions calmer. In a heavily built-up town or city, the environmental Ch'i does not flow smoothly and this imbalance affects both your own bodily Ch'i and your state of mind.

According to Feng Shui, by changing the layout of our environment and homes, we can encourage the Ch'i to flow more freely. This encourages our bodily Ch'i to follow suit and our lives become more tranquil, healthy, prosperous and altogether more satisfying.

YIN AND YANG

Yin and Yang are the names given to what you might consider the polarities of Ch'i. Just as water can be hot or cold, so the Ch'i energy in your home and environment can be Yin or Yang. Unlike true polarities, however, nothing can ever be totally Yin or Yang. One will always contain a small element of the other. Consider the following illustration of the classic Yin/Yang symbol:

The dark half of the symbol represents the Yin of energy. This is considered to be the feminine side of energy and represents tranquillity. Within the Yin is a small element of Yang, however, represented by the light dot.

The light half of the symbol represents the Yang of energy. This is considered to be the masculine side of energy and represents action. Again, within the Yang there is a small element of Yin, represented by the dark dot.

As a whole, the symbol represents the perfect balance of the universe where there is as much Yin as Yang. Night follows day. Autumn and winter follow spring and summer. Instinctively, human beings strive to maintain this sense of balance in their own lives. We try to balance the Yang of work with the Yin of rest and relaxation.

We aim to counter the Yin of contemplation with the Yang of taking action. We seek to do 'all things in moderation', and avoid the trap of leaning excessively in one direction or the other.

Unfortunately, in many homes and offices no such balance of Yin and Yang exists, and where a natural leaning to either Yin or Yang would be desirable, the balance is often tipped detrimentally in the opposite direction.

Let's look at this in more detail. An office is a place where people gather with one aim in mind: to work together to generate greater levels of wealth for all concerned. Because this requires action rather than contemplation, an office should lean towards Yang. It should be bright and angular, since these are Yang qualities which would stimulate everyone to work hard and get things done. Very often, however, offices do not lean towards Yang; they lean towards Yin, with poor lighting and less angles. This lulls everyone into a classic Yin mode of relaxing, so goals are not met and wealth is not generated as quickly as it should be. If this continues over an extended period, the whole business could collapse, simply because Yin has been allowed to become the more dominant polarity.

The same thing happens in our homes. Home is primarily the place where we should feel safe, secure and able to relax. These are Yin qualities, so ambient lighting and curves rather than angles are desirable. Many homes, however, lean towards the opposite polarity, Yang. Lights are too bright, angled furniture abounds and the residents find it difficult to sit down and relax with each other. Instead everyone adopts the Yang quality of action and begins 'doing their own thing'. Family members are seldom in the same place at the same time, and even when they are they can never relax enough to enjoy each other's company. Over an extended period of time this might result in the collapse of the family unit altogether.

One goal of Feng Shui is to correct these imbalances and ensure that Yin and Yang are perfectly balanced or that the leaning towards one polarity is desirable. This helps individuals to take action when they need to and to relax when they don't. The end result will be a more productive business life and a more enjoyable home life. Success and satisfaction in one area will automatically lead to success and satisfaction in another.

THE ENVIRONMENT

As we said earlier, there is a clear link between the flow of Ch'i in the environment and in the lives of individuals. This link works in two ways, and understanding both is vital if you want to get the very best results possible from your work with Feng Shui.

The environment as a mirror

Walk into the home of any stranger and before you have even been introduced to the owner you will get a strikingly accurate snapshot of their life and experience just by looking at what surrounds you. If all you see is chaos, you may well surmise that the owner is finding life difficult at the moment and is burdened with a similar sense of inner chaos. If, on the other hand, you see a home which is ordered and gives an impression of balance and stability, it is likely that the owner is currently enjoying a life of relative order and inner peace.

This simple example serves to illustrate that the environment of an individual is often a reflection of what that individual is experiencing in their day-to-day life. The environment can therefore be considered as something of a mirror, and like all mirrors, it can give you a clear view of what – if anything – needs to be changed.

Take a look at your own home and try to be as objective as possible. Imagine that you have stepped into someone else's house and you are trying to gain an insight into the state of the owner's life. Does what you see indicate a life of order, tranquillity, balance and satisfaction? Or is the place more chaotic, suggesting that life is not as balanced as it could be? How do your insights compare with reality as you know it?

Take a look at how the seating is arranged in the living room. Do people sit directly opposite one another? This could indicate that there is a lot of conflict in a relationship. Do people sit side by side, making it difficult to face each other? This could indicate little communication between family members. Or do people sit at an angle to one another? This could indicate good relationships, with little confrontation and healthy communication.

Now look at the kitchen, where food is prepared which allows the family to go out and generate wealth and prosperity. Is the kitchen clean, tidy and ordered? If so, this indicates that family finances are equally ship-shape. Or is the kitchen cluttered and untidy, with dirty dishes waiting to be washed? This indicates that family finances are not very well organised and that matters are often left until the last minute before being dealt with.

As you will see more fully in later chapters, each room in your house governs a different area of your life. Your kitchen and bathroom govern wealth, your living room governs family life and your bedroom governs emotional health and close relationships. Look at each room in turn and ask yourself how each mirrors your experience in each of these areas. Can you see any correlations?

Now think about how each of these rooms have changed over the last year. Does your kitchen feel more or less balanced and ordered than it did a year ago? In the light of this, how has your financial situation changed over the same period?

What most people find is that if they are struggling with one particular area in life (such as finances) then the rooms in their home which govern this area (the kitchen and bathroom) reflect this struggle. Show me a balanced and tranquil kitchen and I will show you a person who has his or her financial life under control. Show me a kitchen which is visually chaotic and I will show you a person who is struggling either to make ends meet or to handle the money they already have.

Once you get used to the idea that your environment reflects your life, you can immediately highlight areas which need attention. This will help you to set priorities as to which rooms in your home need urgent Feng Shui attention, and in doing so ensure that the related part of your life is improved as quickly as possible.

The environment as an inducer

As well as mirroring our lives, the environment also creates or induces experiences which we may or may not find desirable. This is because – as we have already seen – environmental Ch'i influences the balance of our personal Ch'i. Consider the following situation:

When an individual's bodily Ch'i is out of balance and they feel tense, nervous or stressed, common sense dictates that the best thing they can do is put themselves in a more natural environment. They instinctively want to take long walks or perhaps a holiday in the countryside or beside the ocean. Doing this exposes the bodily Ch'i to the perfect balance of the environmental Ch'i in a natural, unspoiled place, and as a result the tension, nerves and anxieties will decrease considerably. Thus the environmental Ch'i induces a change in the life experience of the individual.

In the same way, someone who is feeling lethargic and drained of personal energy (both of which are classic symptoms of excessive Yin), may immediately begin to feel better if they put themselves in an environment which has a lot of Yang energy, such as a rock concert, party or cinema. All these environments have a strong element of action which stimulates the Ch'i of the individual, encouraging a greater level of personal energy.

The lesson: change your environment, change your life

The conclusion drawn from these examples is that if you want to change your life, you should change your environment. As your life becomes more balanced, so your environment will mirror this balance. The link between the environment and the individual is two-fold, with each having a distinct effect on the other.

Feng Shui aims to change our lives by first changing the environments in which we spend the majority of our time. Practitioners know that the first step to restoring a sense of balance in the life of an individual is to create a sense of balance in the home. When that balance has been restored the environment will continue reflecting this harmonious state, and a circle of tranquillity is created.

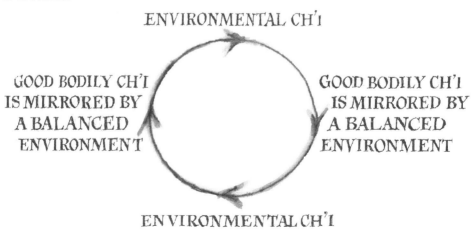

ENVIRONMENTAL CH'I

GOOD BODILY CH'I IS MIRRORED BY A BALANCED ENVIRONMENT

GOOD BODILY CH'I IS MIRRORED BY A BALANCED ENVIRONMENT

ENVIRONMENTAL CH'I

The results of such carefully engineered balance can be truly extraordinary. Businessmen and women have found that implementing Feng Shui in their offices has helped generate tremendous increases in productivity and demand for their products or services. People suffering from poor marital relationships have found that implementing Feng Shui in their homes has helped revolutionise both their sex lives and their ability to communicate with their partners. Others who have struggled to make ends meet financially have discovered that Feng Shui can help inject great wealth into their lives.

THE PERVASIVENESS OF ENERGY

When many people encounter Feng Shui for the first time they wonder how on earth something as apparently simple as changing the appearance of a room or home can possibly help to improve their lives. Such people are often unwilling to accept talk of Ch'i energy without question. Instead they want proof that such an energy exists, and for many years that proof has been lacking.

For thousands of years scientists made distinctions between matter and unseen energy. Matter, they insisted, could be experienced through the five senses. You could touch it, smell it, taste it, see it and if you dropped it, you could hear it. Unseen energy, because it was not 'provable' to the five senses, was considered secondary to matter. Spiritual and metaphysical practitioners of all persuasions were therefore approached, if approached at all, with much scepticism.

Later developments led the scientific community to discover that matter is not as solid as it may appear, but is actually made up of molecules and atoms which vibrate at certain rates. In gases the vibration is quite slow, in liquids it is much faster, and in solid objects the vibration is much faster still. The distinctions between matter and unseen energy were beginning to break down.

Now quantum physics has led scientists to believe what metaphysical teachers have been saying since time began, that matter is nothing more than a manifestation of energy. This book, your body, the clothes you are wearing, are all manifestations of the same energy. Suddenly quantum scientists are saying there is no real 'separateness' in the universe, but that everything is connected because everything is a part of the one energy: universal energy. In much the same way that each drop of water in an ocean is part of that one ocean, on a quantum level you and I and everyone else are part of the same being, because we share the same energy.

Because everything in the universe is merely a manifestation of this one energy, what happens to one particular part of that energy can have major effects on the rest of it. A supernova on one side of the universe can change the physical make-up of our own solar system. A butterfly moving its wings on one side of the planet can cause a hurricane on the opposite side.

This is the basic foundation of Feng Shui: that small changes made to your environment can have dramatic effects on the whole of your life; not because of superstition or heresy, but because it actually changes the state of the energy which flows around, through and in you. In other words, it changes the state of the energy which *is* you.

2

THE PRINCIPLES
The 'Universal Rules'

Now you have been introduced to the main philosophies and beliefs on which Feng Shui is based, let's briefly discuss what are commonly referred to as 'Universal Rules'. These include what are known as the 'Basic Cures' of Feng Shui, which can be applied, to a large extent, to any room in your home with good results. In subsequent chapters we will use all these universal rules to achieve specific results, but for now my aim is simply to present you with an overview of them so that applying them later will be as straightforward as possible.

THE COMPASS POINTS

Traditionally it is said that Ch'i energy has different qualities in different directions. By being aware of these qualities in relation to the compass points, the question of what piece of furniture should go where is largely elementary. Here are the eight compass points plus the centre-point which are referred to throughout the book.

To find out how these compass points relate to your own home, use a compass and make a note of magnetic north. Then sketch a rough plan of your house and superimpose the compass points. A completed sketch might look something like this (see below).

Having a sketch such as this allows you to decide which rooms in your home are best suited for which purpose or individual. Whilst in many cases it is not possible to move the location of a particular room without extensive structural refurbishment (moving a kitchen from one side of the building to the other, for example), it is often possible to allocate bedrooms or work rooms to different members of the family according to their personalities, goals and corresponding Feng Shui energy.

Let's now briefly discuss the major definition of each compass point in relation to the energy of that direction, and provide you with both the colour and the element associated with it. All this information will help you decide which rooms in your home are best suited to a particular person or purpose.

NORTH

Element : **Water**   *Colour* : **Black**

Northern energy is associated with tranquillity, relaxation and sexual relationships. This makes the northern section of the house an ideal site for a main bedroom where you can expect a stable sex life and a peaceful, contented relationship with your partner. This is also a good zone in which to spend time in spiritual studies or meditation, and is seen by many as the most conducive to receiving inner guidance and developing extra-sensory awareness. In addition, the 'awakening' quality of northern energy is helpful to those people who are looking to make a change in their lives, career or other areas.

NORTH

TRANQUILLITY

SEX

CAREER

BLACK

WATER

NORTH-EAST

Element : **Earth**   *Colour* : **Blue**

NORTH·EAST

MOTIVATION

PURPOSE

KNOWLEDGE

BLUE

EARTH

The energy of the north-east is strong on instilling a sense of motivation and purpose. Spending time in this zone can help an individual clarify their goals and ambitions and give them the emotional drive to attain them. It helps stimulate knowledge, both of oneself and of the world in general. It is therefore a good energy for those people who need to be clear about their direction in life, such as students and job-seekers. Because of the strong motivational factors associated with this energy, the north-east is also a good place for both adults and children to play games or undertake physical exercise. A home gymnasium or playroom would therefore do well in this section of the home.

EAST

Element : **Wood**   *Colour* : **Green**

Eastern energy instils a sense of contentment and optimism. It is a good site for the bedroom of someone who is usually restless or pessimistic because the energy of this zone will help to change their outlook on life to one which is more positive. The whole 'feel' of this energy encourages an individual to look forward and plan the future in a more positive frame of mind. It is therefore of benefit to anyone feeling

EAST

CONTENTMENT

OPTIMISM

HEALTH

GREEN

WOOD

dispirited about their prospects and needing a boost of positive energy. This zone also helps people to enjoy good levels of health, so sleeping here could be beneficial to someone feeling generally below par. Other rooms which suit this area are kitchens, studies and home offices, in which cases the energy will again foster a mood of optimism about the future.

SOUTH-EAST

Element : **Wood**   *Colour :* **Purple**

SOUTH-EAST

WEALTH

CREATIVITY

PURPLE

WOOD

The south-east is associated with wealth and creativity in all its forms. Individuals who have a study or office in this area will enjoy a gradual yet steady build-up of wealth and success in their business. A bedroom in this area also encourages financial success. Creativity is stimulated in all areas of that person's life, and they will therefore often find new ways to solve stubborn problems or make the most of their natural gifts and abilities. Since both wealth and creativity are also associated with the kitchen, this is a particularly good area in which to prepare food. Placing a kitchen in this region greatly enhances the value of the zonal energies.

SOUTH

Element : Fire   **Colour : Red**

Southern energy is very conducive to success and the attainment of a high social or public profile. This makes the southern part of a house ideal for a dining room where entertaining guests will be both enjoyable and beneficial for all concerned. People who are in business and entertain potential or existing clients and business associates will want to take advantage of this strong energy. Having a bedroom in this area may suit those who wish to

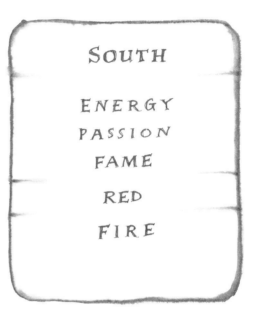

SOUTH

ENERGY
PASSION
FAME
RED
FIRE

become famous, but sleeping in such a fiery energy can often be difficult. The energy of the south is also conducive to passion, however, so if an individual's sex life is lacking zest, using this room will help re-ignite the spark of physical hunger. In this case, lack of sleep will not be too much of a problem!

▶ MODERN LOUNGE

The first thing you will notice, as you look in from the door, is that this modern lounge has very little clutter, and this allows the Ch'i to circulate easily, with positive benefits. The chair positioned in the centre of the room, however, will disrupt this flow and would be better situated in a more unobtrusive area, leaving the central zone free. This has the most advantages for the family's health and general well-being.

The standard lamp brightens a potentially dark corner without flooding the whole room with artificial light, and this will help the occupants to relax after a long day at work. Keeping the curtains well back from the windows allows the maximum natural light to enter the room.

The sofa should be moved to give the occupants a direct view of the door, or if this is not possible, a mirror hung to provide a reflected view.

Finally, the room would benefit from more colour. Coloured furnishings should be added according to which zones the occupants particularly wish to stimulate. The red table, for example, could be positioned in the south section of the room to stimulate the energies in the home, or more colour added in the way of pictures, curtains or soft furnishings such as cushions.

▶ FAMILY LOUNGE

This family lounge has a lot of central space, which is good for Ch'i flow. This will have positive benefits on the health of the family.

The mirror hung on the wall above the fireplace provides further Ch'i stimulation and also serves to reflect light from the window in the north-east. Since the sofa is not in the ideal position facing the door, from where the photograph is taken, the mirror also fulfills the additional role of providing a reflected view of the doorway.

The television in the northern corner is ideally situated to stimulate the energy governing tranquillity, sex and career, so one could expect the occupants to be particularly satisfied in these respects.

Light curtains encourage plenty of natural light into the room. Some additional wall lighting or small table or standard lamps would allow the occupants more control over the light levels in the room so that they can adjust the atmosphere to be more or less restful or stimulating.

One advantage might be gained by moving the blue chair to the opposite side of the room – ideally in the north-eastern zone relating to motivation and purpose, which is more suited to blue colours. This would help to enhance the family's sense of general direction in their lives.

◀ EDWARDIAN SITTING ROOM

Plants and a mirror have been carefully used in this very stylish room to keep the Ch'i flowing smoothly throughout. The soft, Yin quality of the sofa and cushions contrasts nicely with the more angular fireplace, but the contrast would be even greater if lighter-coloured cushions were used, since these would give a 'lift' to the darker sofa. The mirror also gives a good reflected view of the door to those sitting on the sofa.

Since the room is in the north-eastern zone of the house, the use of the strong blue-green colours strengthens the Ch'i relating to both areas.

The windows in this room are generously large, allowing a good quantity of solar Ch'i to enter. Also, the light is not blocked or impeded by heavy curtains.

The photographs on the mantelpiece give the room a very personal touch, but the occupants should try to avoid cluttering any one surface. The photos should therefore be spread throughout the room fairly evenly, as this will ensure that they do not slow down the flow of Ch'i too much.

When the fireplace is not in use, a plant could be placed in front of it. Ch'i can linger around a dark fireplace, but a plant would provide good stimulation and keep the Ch'i flow smooth.

◀ LIGHT AND STYLISH SITTING ROOM

This is a very stylish sitting room, but there are a few Feng Shui problems which need attention. The fire is situated in the southern zone, which is a good position to maximise energies and passion. However, the black etchings above the fire would be more beneficial if moved to the opposite side of the room, since black is associated with water and the opposing zone. Repositioning them would give more stimulation to the areas of tranquillity, sex and careers, which are governed by the northern zone.

The use of plants is good, bringing life into the room, and the soft furnishings contrast nicely with the more angular furnishings, balancing the levels of Yin and Yang. Plenty of natural light is encouraged through the large windows and light-coloured curtains, and the clear central area allows a positive free flow of Ch'i.

The open bookshelves which can be seen on the right of the picture and extend on to the southern wall can create harmful Ch'i daggers which may make occupants feel restless and tense. To avoid this, the shelves would benefit from the fitting of glass doors.

SOUTH-WEST

Element : **Earth**   *Colour* : **Pink**

> SOUTH-WEST
>
> TRANQUILLITY
> RELATIONSHIPS
> PRACTICALITY
>
> PINK
>
> EARTH

The energy of the south-west is one of tranquillity and is particularly helpful in building and maintaining strong relationships. A family which has its living or dining room in this area will have few serious quarrels, but will enjoy a stable home base which feels both protective and safe. A bedroom in this area will provide a very warm and comfortable environment on an emotional level. Another aspect of this energy is that it encourages practicality. Problems of all kinds are easily solved in this area, perhaps because the strong relationships it creates generates a firm underlying trust and understanding between family members, which makes communication easier.

WEST

Element : **Metal**   ## Colour : **White**

Western energy is associated with a deep sense of love between family members, and with the overall prosperity of the family unit. Having a dining or living room in this area will therefore help to ensure that family bonds are strong and also that material hardships are kept to a minimum. A family experiencing communication or relationship problems could therefore do well to focus their living area in this zone of the home in order to benefit from

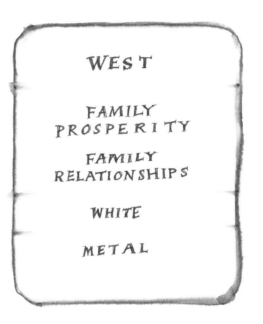

this ch'i energy. Children's or young people's bedrooms fare well here because the energy makes children feel loved and safe. This helps to temper the effects of any emotional difficulties they may face in childhood, at school or as they progress towards adulthood.

NORTH-WEST

Element : **Metal**   *Colour* : **Grey**

NORTH·WEST

RESPONSIBILITY

PLANNING

LEADERSHIP

GREY

METAL

The north-western zone's dominating energy governs aspects such as responsibility and the ability to plan, organise and lead. This affects both social circles and business. It is therefore an ideal site for a study or home office, as the person working there will optimise the energies supporting them in their work. It is also an advantageous situation for the bedroom of someone who would like to excel in these areas. Employees who are feeling frustrated because they do not believe they are being given the level of responsibility they deserve may also find that sleeping in this area of the home helps to change their situation. Sleeping in the north-western zone of the house may also benefit those who are trying to reassess and reorganise their social life to better advantage.

CENTRE

Element : **Earth**   Colour : **Yellow**

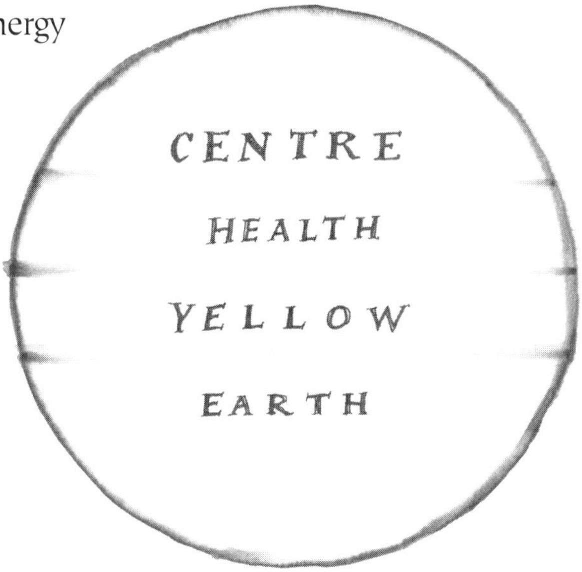

By far the most powerful energy can be found in the central zone. The energy here is associated with good physical, spiritual and emotional health, although aspects of the eight directional energies can also be found in this area. If the central zone of a home or individual room is blocked with furniture then the health of people in the household may not be as good as it could be. The best thing is to leave this area as free of clutter as possible; the more open the space the better. This makes the central zone ideal for a hallway.

CENTRE

HEALTH

YELLOW

EARTH

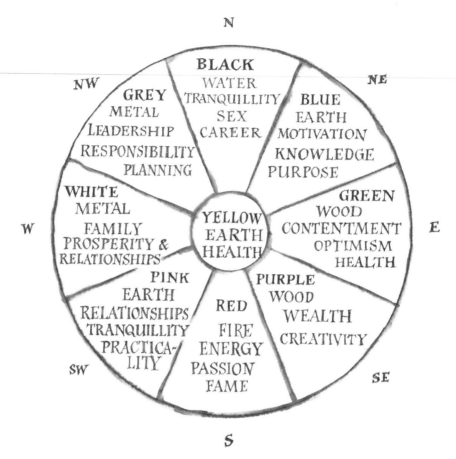

To sum up ...

By examining these directional energy associations you can determine, for example, where to situate a home office, master bedroom or dining room. If moving rooms is not possible all is not lost; the power of Feng Shui can still be applied with excellent results. The fact is that very few homes are designed with Feng Shui in mind and so perfection, although preferable, is seldom attainable. Later chapters will show you how to make improvements to every room in your home even if it is not possible to site them in the 'perfect' compass position. In the meantime, let us put all the compass point information on to one chart so that you can see at a glance the qualities of each direction.

SHAPES

Some shapes are more beneficial than others from a Feng Shui point of view. Simple shapes such as squares, rectangles and circles are best for both individual rooms and an entire building. In practice, however, both buildings and the rooms within them have more complicated shapes. L-shaped rooms, such as the one illustrated below, are common.

Because there appears to be a 'missing' section of the room, the energy of this missing direction will be very weak. In this illustration the north-east section of the room is missing, and since the north-west governs motivation, knowledge and purpose, residents of this room may find that their lives lack the same qualities. To compensate for the 'missing' section of the room, a mirror can be hung on the opposite wall (as illustrated). This

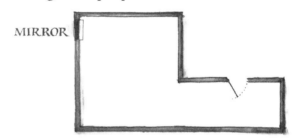

creates the impression of wholeness and encourages the Ch'i energy of the north-eastern section of the room to behave just as it would in a more desirable rectangular room.

A mirror could be hung opposite the door to achieve the same effect.

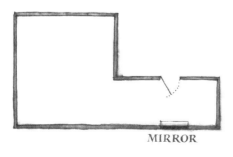

We will be looking at how shapes can be applied to particular situations when we tackle each room individually. Until then, simply bear in mind that regular shapes such as squares, rectangles and circles are more beneficial than any others.

DOORS

No matter what room they are in, one of the universal principles of Feng Shui is that the occupant must always be able to see the door.

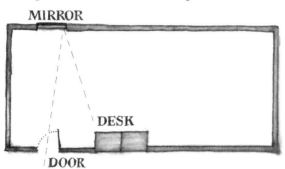

This probably stems from the fact that in ancient times individuals were constantly on their guard and didn't want to be surprised by enemies, but the principle is still applicable today.

Occasionally it may not be possible to place your desk or sofa – in other words the place you are most likely to be sitting – in a position where you can see the door. If this is the case a mirror can be hung so you can at least see the reflection of the door and be aware of anyone who enters unannounced.

WINDOWS

Windows are also important in Feng Shui, because they allow solar Ch'i to enter the room in the form of daylight. In general, the larger the windows the better, because even if too much light enters a room (for example, there may be too much light in a bedroom, making it difficult for the occupier to sleep), then solving this problem is simply a matter of hanging a pair of heavy curtains or a thick blind.

Small windows are a different matter altogether. If a room has a small window then a large mirror should be hung alongside it so that as much light as possible is reflected into the room. By doing this, even rooms which are usually dark can receive a greater amount of solar Ch'i. We will look at this use of mirrors a little later in this chapter.

'BASIC CURES'

'Basic cures' are methods commonly used by Feng Shui practitioners to help stimulate and lift the Ch'i energy of a home. Classically, they include the following: light, mirrors, crystals, sound, life (living things), movement, electricity, colour and water.

Light

Light is very important in Feng Shui and can be used in a number of ways to enhance any room. Natural light is to be encouraged wherever possible. The sun radiates its own unique Ch'i, which can dramatically affect the atmosphere of any environment. This is why people often feel emotionally happier and more content on bright, sunny days than they do on cloudy or dull days. You should consider avoiding dark-coloured curtains since these can absorb natural light even when open. Light-coloured curtains – such as cream or beige – will reflect natural light into the home and can help to lift the feeling of a whole room. Blinds are often more beneficial than curtains, since during daylight hours they can be rolled up, allowing the maximum amount of natural light to enter a room.

Rooms in which you want a lot of activity should be brightly lit, because light is a visible manifestation of Yang energy; the more Yang energy in a room, the more active it will be. Active Yang energy can be encouraged by the installation of bright spotlights. For example, a bright spotlight over a desk will help a person focus on the job in hand and get things done.

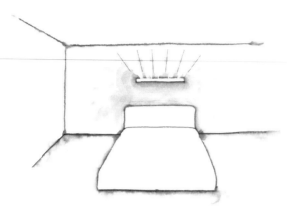

Rooms in which you want to sleep should be more Yin, so bright lights are out of the question and a more subdued ambience should be created. This can be achieved with wall lights which illuminate the ceiling but do not directly illuminate the lower section of the room.

Other rooms which are to be used for both rest and play should have a balance of light and shade. This creates a balance of Yin and Yang and promotes an atmosphere of tranquillity and peace which is suitable for most purposes. Installing a dimmer switch in these rooms will enable you to adjust the level of lighting according to the activity you want to use it for.

Light is particularly important in homes which have low ceilings or a lot of dark corners. Spotlights aimed at low ceilings lift the Ch'i of a room and can be most beneficial. Lamps or even candles can counter the Yin of dark corners and stimulate the often slow-moving Ch'i of these areas.

Mirrors

Mirrors are used a great deal in Feng Shui. As you have already seen, one use of mirrors is to compensate for or 'balance' a room which has an irregular shape. Another is to give you a reflected view of the door in any room. This, however, is just the tip of the iceberg, and mirrors can be used in many other ways.

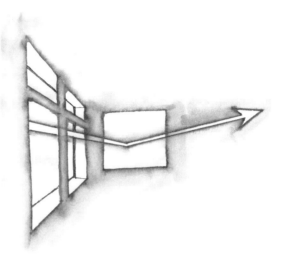

They can be hung beside windows to attract more natural light and Ch'i into the room.

If the reflected image is one of nature (trees, mountains or water, for example) then so much the better, since these will also generate a more beneficial energy into the room.

Mirrors can also be used to give the impression of more space in an otherwise cramped room. A small bathroom, for example, can be made to feel twice as large if a sizeable mirror is hung on an appropriate wall.

Crystals

Crystals have long been considered 'the batteries of nature'. They are said to have an excellent capacity for storing energy and their healing qualities are legendary. In Feng Shui, crystals are used both to balance negative Ch'i and to stimulate the positive.

Because they act as prisms which refract light, crystals can be placed or hung in front of windows so more natural light is attracted into a room. This is especially beneficial in rooms which do not receive as much natural light as one might hope for. The size of crystal you use is entirely up to you. Large crystals will obviously refract more natural light than smaller ones, and have pleasing ornamental value. Smaller crystals are better suited for hanging and will tend to sway from side to side in any breeze, stimulating the surrounding Ch'i energy still further.

Sound

We have talked about how light, being a visible manifestation of energy, is important to Feng Shui. So too is sound, because it is an auditory manifestation of the same energy. The vibrations caused by any sound have an effect on the Ch'i energy around them. Stark, rasping sounds send Ch'i energy in all directions, dramatically obstructing the regular flow it is used to and creating an environment which is never very beneficial to the people in it. Clear, simple sounds, on the other hand, have the effect of stimulating the Ch'i energy without disrupting its flow.

For this reason, Feng Shui practitioners use wind chimes to stimulate Ch'i beneficially. Almost any wind chime will have the desired effect, but metal ones are preferable since the vibratory frequencies that these produce are the most productive. Wind chimes can be hung in any area where you would deliberately like to stimulate Ch'i.

If a chime is hung in the southern part of a room, for example, the southern energy associated with passion and the public and social profile of an individual will be stimulated; this could help you enjoy more satisfying physical relationships or higher recognition in social and business circles. In the same way, if you wanted to experience a greater level of creativity and wealth, you would hang a chime in the south-eastern part of a room, which governs these qualities. Think about the areas of your life which most need stimulation and position your chimes accordingly.

Life (living things)

Because living things radiate a particularly strong Ch'i which is beneficial to an environment, bringing them into your home can bring good Ch'i. Placing plants around the home is one of the easiest ways of generating such energy, but you must ensure that you look after them well. Plants which have dead leaves on them or are otherwise lacking in health symbolise decay and bring bad Ch'i into the home.

If you don't have green fingers the answer may be to bring some artificial plants into your home. These symbolise the Ch'i of life and can often be almost as effective as the real thing, but because they do not live and 'breathe' they will not stimulate the surrounding Ch'i as much as living plants. The main benefit of using artificial plants is that they need a minimum of maintenance; all that is required is a weekly or fortnightly dusting so they look as 'fresh' as possible.

The type of plant you use in a room depends largely on whether you want to encourage a greater level of Yin or Yang energy. Plants which have angular or spiky leaves are Yang and will tend to make a room more beneficial to those who wish to be active. Plants with smooth, more rounded leaves are Yin and will contribute to a more relaxing atmosphere.

Plants can be placed almost anywhere and benefit the overall energy of a room. Placing them in particular sections of the room, however, can bring dramatic results. A Yang plant in the south-eastern corner of a home office will help to increase the wealth and creativity of the worker. In the same way a Yin plant placed in the western section of a living room will encourage better family relationships.

Another popular way of bringing life into the home is to establish a simple aquarium. As long as the fish are healthy and the aquarium is kept as clean as possible, very good Ch'i will be released into a room. Many restaurateurs in China establish an aquarium on their premises to help generate a good flow of custom and increase their prosperity. Again, an aquarium will be beneficial to some degree regardless of where it is situated, but for the best effect it should be placed in a part of the room which you particularly want to stimulate.

Movement

Movement stimulates beneficial Ch'i energy and helps break up any harmful Ch'i. For this reason many Feng Shui practitioners hang mobiles in areas which may be helpful to the resident, such as the north-western corner of a room to improve matters relating to organisation and leadership, or the south-western section to encourage better relationships and practicality.

Other items which move can be used as a substitute for or in addition to a mobile – for example, a small battery- or mains-operated windmill.

Clocks are particularly good for bringing an element of movement into a room. The type of clock you use is largely a matter of personal taste, but make sure the movement is visible, as is the case with a swinging pendulum or sweeping second hand.

As with mobiles and windmills, clocks should be positioned in the part of a room which you particularly want to stimulate. A clock in the southern section of a room will encourage a greater level of passion and energy in your life; a clock in the northern section of a room will stimulate the energy which governs your sex life and career.

Electricity

Electrical appliances are also used to help stimulate Ch'i in a room. Placing a television or computer in the south-eastern part of a room will aid the generation of wealth and increase the level of creativity enjoyed by the occupant, because the energy given out by the appliance will improve the Ch'i energy surrounding it. In the same way, other areas can be stimulated by moving an electrical appliance to the corresponding compass zone.

For example, placing a radio in the southern part of a room will help increase your energy levels, whilst a television in the eastern zone will stimulate the Ch'i which governs your health and mental outlook on life.

Colour

We have already assigned certain colours to the eight directions and centre-point which we discussed at the beginning of this chapter. These can be applied throughout your home and adjustments made for taste, etc. The colours relate to the element which dominates that zone; those belonging to opposing elements should be avoided if possible.

For example, a room in the south of your home should contain fire colours such as red, orange and perhaps pinks and purples. The opposing element to fire is water (which belongs to the northern zone), so blacks, greys and blues should be avoided.

This does not mean the whole of a room must be red or orange; this would not suit most people's taste! These colours can be established by using vibrant paintings, scatter cushions, and so on, whilst the rest of the room may be more subtle in colour. We will look at the use of specific colours when we tackle each room individually, but for now use the compass colours as a guide.

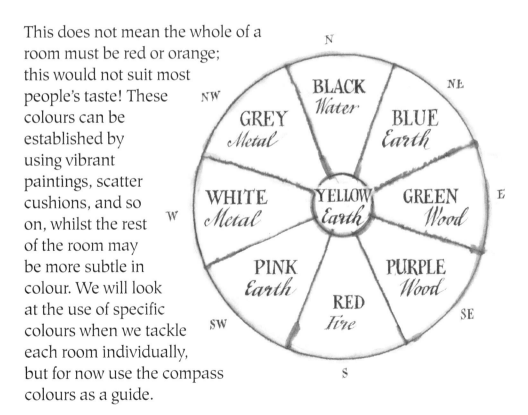

Water

Water covers over two-thirds of the planet. It also makes up the same proportion of our physical bodies. Perhaps this is why water is said to be particularly useful in Feng Shui. Fountains – the perpetual movement of water – when placed in the south-east, can have a dramatic effect in helping a household experience greater levels of financial prosperity and material success. Big businesses have caught on to this fact and many install large fountains either just outside or in the foyer of their premises to help them generate greater levels of profitability.

Of course, not everyone has room for even a small fountain at their home. This is not a great problem, however, since any body of water can bring the same beneficial effects. An aquarium brings both life and water into the home, and even a bowl of water with a floating candle will stimulate the Ch'i energy which surrounds it, so anyone can harness the beneficial energy of water by bringing it indoors.

One thing you must avoid is allowing any body of water to become dirty or stagnant. Water which is not fresh can adversely affect the surrounding Ch'i and cause more harm than good. Clean water in the south-west would improve tranquillity in relationships, but dirty or stagnant water in the same position would be more likely to disrupt any existing tranquillity. Remember to keep any body of water clean and fresh at all times, and stagnation and negative Ch'i will not be a problem.

CREATING A HOUSE PLAN

From the next chapter on we will be discussing the application of Feng Shui on a room-by-room basis. To make this as straightforward as possible, sketch a plan of each room in your home and superimpose the compass points. This is important because even if the whole of a room is contained in the northern area of the home, it will still have aspects of the other directions.

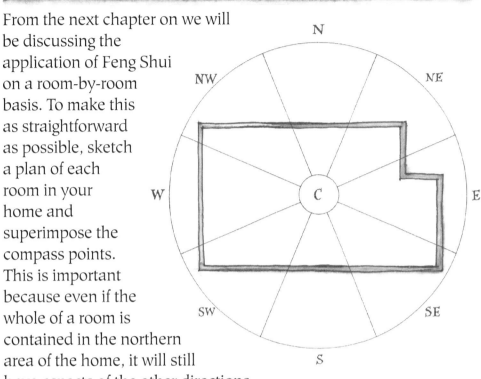

Your sketch might look something like this (see right).

Once you have drawn up a sketch for each room in your home, we can start applying detailed Feng Shui solutions so that the energy in your environment starts working *for* you rather than *against* you. We will begin with the lounge.

3

THE LOUNGE

T he lounge in any home is the place where families spend substantial amounts of time together. It is where relationships are forged and problems solved. It is a place where the stresses and strains of everyday life can be forgotten, and so many people see it as a personal refuge from the outside world. The lounge should therefore be as conducive to relaxation and harmony as possible, so that the relationships developed and sustained within it are pleasant and enjoyable.

THE DOOR

The entrance to the lounge will automatically create a slight imbalance of Ch'i no matter where it is. The quality of Ch'i which is affected will depend on where the entrance is in relation to the compass zones we discussed earlier.

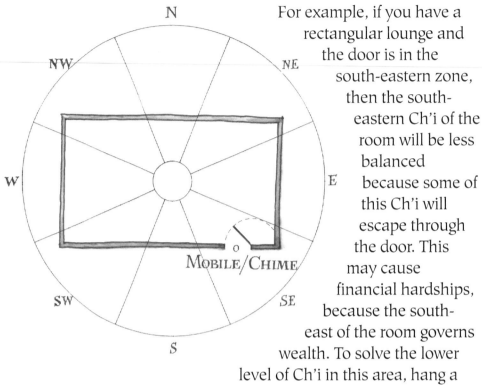

For example, if you have a rectangular lounge and the door is in the south-eastern zone, then the south-eastern Ch'i of the room will be less balanced because some of this Ch'i will escape through the door. This may cause financial hardships, because the south-east of the room governs wealth. To solve the lower level of Ch'i in this area, hang a mobile or wind chime above the door, as illustrated.

If the door to the lounge is in another zone, the same principle holds true. The zone will suffer from a slightly unbalanced level of Ch'i energy, and this should be countered by hanging a mobile or chime over the doorway.

Once that has been dealt with, we can begin solving some of the fundamental problems which many lounges present.

ALCOVES

When part of one wall in the room protrudes from the rest at least one alcove is created, and this can slow down the Ch'i circulation in that part of the room. For example, if a chimney breast protrudes from the rest of a northern wall, an alcove will be created in both the north-western and north-eastern zones. This will result in a lessened ability to lead and plan, since these are governed by north-western Ch'i, and in a lower sense of motivation and purpose, because these qualities are governed by north-eastern Ch'i.

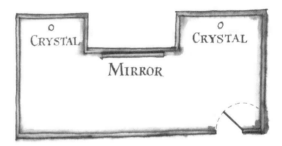

To solve this problem, wherever it exists, you should place a crystal in each alcove and a mirror on the protruding part of the wall. The crystals will help to stimulate the Ch'i in the alcoves and the mirror will help to give the protruding wall a feeling of depth, as illustrated.

OPEN-PLAN ROOMS

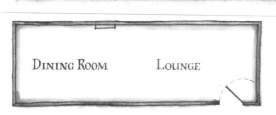

If two rooms meet in an open-plan arrangement, the Ch'i in some zones will be lower in quality than if the rooms were self-contained.

In this illustration the dining room and lounge merge in an open-plan arrangement and there is no real element of 'separateness' between the two. The north-western, western and south-western zones of the lounge are not apparent, and this means that three vital types of directional Ch'i energy are also missing. At the same time the dining room does not appear to have the north-eastern, eastern or south-eastern zones, so three different vital energies are also missing from that room.

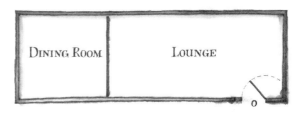

The solution is to artificially divide the two rooms with a screen (as above). This will restore the three 'missing' compass points to each room and balance will be restored.

CEILINGS

The ceiling in any room is very important, but in the lounge it is even more so. Ch'i bounces off the ceiling and back down to the people below, so if the ceiling is not uniform the rebounding Ch'i can have negative connotations.

Take, for example, a beamed ceiling. Beams give a very traditional and warming 'feel' to a room, but they disrupt Ch'i quite badly and their square edges can reflect the energy towards the residents very sharply. This almost always creates an uncomfortable feeling and most people find it hard to relax under this harsh reflection.

Slanted ceilings pose much the same problem. Ch'i is reflected back from the ceiling at awkward angles, creating an uncomfortable atmosphere which can at times feel downright oppressive.

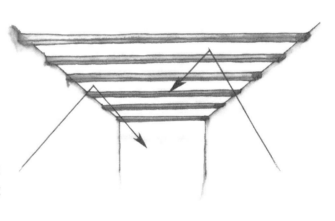

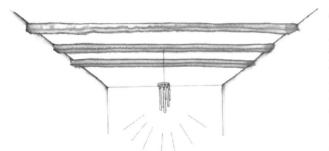

The solution to both problems is to hang a mobile or wind chime from the ceiling to help dissipate any negative Ch'i generated by the beams or slope. This ensures a more balanced distribution of Ch'i, and instead of reflecting harshly down on to the residents it 'rains' down on them much more gently.

THE SUITE

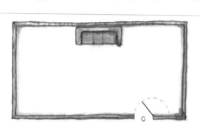

The suite in any lounge should be curved rather than angled. We do not want too much Yang (angles) in the room because this would make it difficult for the occupants to relax. The recent popularity of more angular living-room furniture does not encourage good Feng Shui.

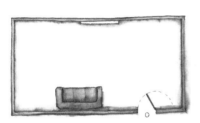

Once you have found a suitable suite, site it, if possible, so the occupants have a full view of the doorway.

If this is not possible a mirror should be hung to reflect the door.

When deciding where to put seats in your home, use some common sense. If seats are placed directly opposite each other this might encourage an atmosphere of 'head-to-head' confrontation.

Since such confrontations are very rarely desirable, a more diagonal or angled arrangement would be better.

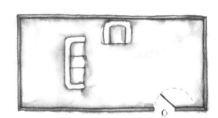

THE FIREPLACE

Many centrally heated homes do not have a fireplace, so if this applies to you, skip this section. If you do have a fireplace in your lounge, follow these rules:

✳ Do not position seats or a sofa so they directly face the fireplace, because this can disrupt the flow of Ch'i in and out of the fireplace itself. Instead, put suites and chairs in a diagonal or 'L-shaped' arrangement.

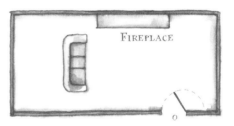

✳ When the fire is not in use, ensure that all ashes are removed and the grate is clean, to allow as much Ch'i circulation as possible.

✳ Place a plant on either side of the fireplace and perhaps one in the fireplace itself when it is not in use. This will ensure that the Ch'i within the fireplace is stimulated even when it is not being used, and will help to maintain balance throughout the room.

THE TELEVISION

Since a television (and video) is an electrical piece of equipment, it should be placed in a zone where you want the Ch'i to be strongly

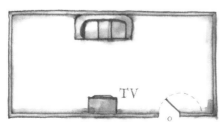

stimulated. Placing your television in the south-eastern section of a room will encourage wealth and prosperity; the south-west will encourage good relationships and practicality; the north-east will encourage a greater sense of motivation and purpose, and so on. In this illustration a television is used to encourage a higher social and business profile by being placed in the southern part of the room.

COFFEE TABLE

Bearing in mind what we have already learnt about the most desirable shapes, these should be circular, rectangular or square. Many people put their coffee table in the centre of the room, but as we said earlier, the central zone of a home or individual rooms should be kept as free of clutter as possible. If you can, put a coffee table to the side of the room and move it to the centre only when it is being used. If you have to have a central coffee table, make sure you put a small vase of fresh flowers on it so the beneficial health Ch'i of the centre is stimulated as much as possible by the life energy of the flowers.

BOOKSHELVES

Because books come in all sorts of different shapes and sizes, books on open shelves can disrupt the flow of the surrounding Ch'i energy quite badly. Because of this, you should aim either to keep bookshelves away from areas of the room where people are sitting or, and this is far more preferable, store books in bookcases which have glass or wooden doors.

DECOR

When decorating your lounge, strive for a balance in all things. Balance angles with curves, shade with light and hard surfaces with fabrics such as scatter cushions. This will help to ensure that Yang is always balanced with Yin, and that the occupants are able to relax fully, leading to better family communication and happiness.

Use soft and subtle colours when decorating the lounge, since these promote greater levels of tranquillity than harsh colours such as bright reds or blues. If you want to bring out the energy of a particular area, for example the wealth energy of the south-east with its related colour red, hang a picture on the southern wall which contains a strong element of this colour. This will provide the desired Ch'i stimulation, but will leave the rest of the room balanced and harmonious.

Pictures of natural landscapes or life (fish swimming, for example) suit this room best, because they symbolise the beneficial Ch'i of nature and help evoke a sense of tranquillity and harmony.

Soft furnishings should be used wherever possible; most lounges benefit from a few subtly-coloured scatter cushions and a softly-coloured thick-pile carpet rather than a rug in a harsher colour. Avoid varnished wooden floors in the lounge; they do not encourage the occupants to relax as fully as they might.

LIGHT

Natural light is to be encouraged as much as possible, so ensure that curtains are always pulled back during daylight hours and aim to attract more light indoors by placing a crystal or mirror by the window. Avoid strong artificial lights, such as fluorescent strips, because these bring a lot of undispersed Yang into the room and will make you feel unduly restless. Instead, consider using standard and table lamps to give the room a relaxed atmosphere in the evenings. This will tend to give the room a greater level of Yin than Yang and will ensure that you and your family recover from the stresses and strains of the day as quickly as possible.

People often get home from a busy day at work and sit under strong artificial lights all through the evening. When they go to bed, they have great difficulty sleeping. The reason is simply that they have spent several hours in a Yang environment, and making the sudden switch to the Yin of sleep is very difficult. Subtle lighting in the lounge will solve this problem almost immediately.

If you wish to stimulate the Ch'i of any particular area, lighting a candle or two in that area will work wonders. A candle in the eastern area of the room will promote greater levels of optimism and health without affecting the balance of the room as a whole. In the same way, a candle in the south-western zone will promote greater levels of tranquillity.

There is an increasing trend for people to use candles purely for decorative purposes, but as far as Feng Shui is concerned candles should be used rather than looked at. It is the candle flame which stimulates the surrounding Ch'i, not the candle itself.

SOUND

Many people complain that there is a lack of communication in their homes. The culprit in these cases is often the television, because all too often it is allowed to remain on in the background when no one is watching anything in particular. The constant stream of sound coming from the television in these situations makes it almost impossible for the Ch'i of the room to settle down, and this makes meaningful communication between occupants very difficult.

To restore some balance to this situation, you should avoid leaving the television on when it is not being watched. This will allow the Ch'i in the room to settle and open the lines of communication between you and the other members of your family.

Background music which is quiet and unobtrusive can be used when you want to help people to relax, but you should try to avoid treating background music or flickering television pictures as a replacement for good communication with others. All too often people find themselves uncomfortable in silence and use sound as a distraction from their thoughts. If these people embraced silence positively, they would begin to develop more peace within themselves, which paradoxically, leads to better communication skills.

▶ TRADITIONAL LOUNGE

This is an excellent traditional lounge from a Feng Shui perspective. The fireplace is in the western zone which governs family relationships, and the metal coal scuttle positioned in front of the fire will help these relationships to improve, since metal is also associated with the west. To top it all, the mirror and dried plants positioned above the fireplace stimulates the Ch'i even further.

The table lamps on either side of the room help to brighten alcoves which might otherwise be prone to slow-moving Ch'i energy and these, together with a small wall light which is used to illuminate a picture, help to ensure that a nice balance between Yin and Yang is maintained.

The seating arrangements are ideal, with occupants sitting at angles to one another in a warm, comfortable setting. Plush cushions and curtains give the room a final touch of softness which will help the occupants to relax and enjoy comfortable, profitable relationships.

◄ COTTAGE LOUNGE WITH STAIRS

The two views of this room show that a major influence is the stairs which go up from the right-hand side by the windows. Whilst this gives the room a good flow of Ch'i from the upper levels of the house, the seating is arranged so that the occupants have their back to the stairs, and this could result in surprise entrances by other people. In situations such as this, where stairs lead directly into a room, the staircase should be treated in the same way as a door. Seating could therefore be arranged so that occupants have a clear view of the staircase or, if this is not possible, a mirror hung to provide a reflected view.

The potentially negative effects of the ceiling beam have been offset with the clever use of ceiling lights which stimulate surrounding Ch'i, and the potentially dark chimney has also been illuminated to transform it into an active feature.

Plants and flowers are well used to bring life into the room and stimulate those sections of the room in which they are placed.

PLANTS

Rubber and cheese plants are ideally suited to the lounge because they have smooth, rounded leaves. When placed in corners of the room they stimulate any slow Ch'i and charge the whole atmosphere with perfectly balanced life and vitality. Potted round-leafed house plants are also very useful. Placing one in front of the window will draw more solar Ch'i into the room, but you must be careful to turn the plant 180 degrees each day so its growth remains as balanced as possible.

Bonsai trees are excellent plants to have in the lounge because they generate a great level of Ch'i which is usually found outdoors. They do, however, have to be tended very carefully if they are to thrive, particularly in centrally-heated atmospheres.

A vase of flowers can bring both life and colour into the lounge, stimulating the Ch'i of its surroundings quite markedly. Positioning a vase of flowers in the southern part of a room can help you develop a more prominent social and business life. A vase of flowers in the western zone, on the other hand, will increase the amount of contentment you experience in life. Think carefully about the placement of the vase to reap the maximum benefit.

If you use vases of flowers in this way, be careful to co-ordinate the colours of the flowers with the compass point colours we discussed earlier. Warm colours such as reds, pinks and purples should be used in the southern half of the room. Colder colours such as turquoise and darker blues should dominate the northern half of the room. The ideal colour for central plants is, of course, yellow.

MOVEMENT

Carriage clocks with visible moving parts are an excellent way of discreetly stimulating Ch'i. Placing one on a mantelpiece or shelf in an area you wish to promote will do the job nicely and – because they provide an element of movement 24 hours each day – ensure constant Ch'i stimulation. A clock in the south will therefore promote greater levels of personal energy, whilst a clock in the north-west will encourage greater levels of responsibility and leadership.

Pendulum clocks are also good for stimulating Ch'i through movement, but can be more difficult to site since they tend to be larger. Consider hanging a medium-sized pendulum clock on the western wall to encourage a greater level of family prosperity and better family relationships.

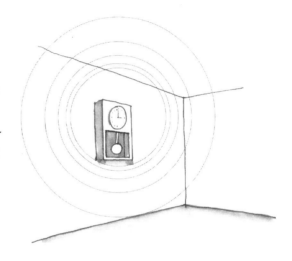

To sum up ...

By applying these simple Feng Shui principles to your lounge you will generate an atmosphere of tranquillity and peace which is as conducive as possible to strong and healthy family relationships.

IMPROVE YOUR LIFESTYLE

How Feng Shui can help you cope with some common problems

Question

Our lounge seems to be the family centre for arguments: who wants to see what on television, who wants to listen to music, who just wants to read, and so on. Feng Shui strategies, please, for lessening family conflict while allowing everyone their rights!

Answer

Arguments in the lounge are usually caused by one of two things: over-stimulation of the fire zone or an excess of Yang caused by having bright artificial lights in the room. Pay attention to the southern fire zone first and make sure that it is not being excessively stimulated by a plant, crystal, electrical appliance or the colour red. If it is, and you can move the object which is stimulating the fire energy, do so. If moving the object is not possible, bring the element of water into the southern zone by introducing the colour black in the form of an ornament, picture or ribbon. This will dampen the fire energy of the south considerably, leading to less passion and so fewer family arguments.

If the room is too bright then the excessive Yang energy created by this may make it difficult for you and your family to relax in each other's company. Arguments can therefore break out quite easily. To guard against this, install a dimmer switch so that artificial lighting can be kept to a more relaxing level. This will reduce the level of Yang in the room and should allow family members to become more relaxed and in harmony with one another.

Question

The children seem to gravitate to the lounge to do their homework, even though they have desks in their bedrooms. How can we use Feng Shui to make the lounge more conducive to productive schoolwork?

Answer

To make homework in the lounge as productive as possible, you should ensure that your children study in the north-eastern zone, which governs knowledge and motivation. The zone should have as much natural light as possible, but when artifical lighting has to be used, a desk lamp which illuminates the working surface directly will be most useful. This will help the children to concentrate on the work before them in a confined Yang atmosphere, but will at the same time guard against the whole of the lounge becoming heavily Yang. The end result should be higher grades without affecting the energy balance of other people in the room.

Question

I find it very difficult to relax in the lounge after a day at work. How can Feng Shui help?

Answer

What you must remember is that a day at work charges you with the active energy of Yang. The only way to relax properly after any kind of activity is to put yourself in an environment which leans further towards the Yin of inactivity. This means making sure that your lounge lights are dim and that external stimulation is as small as possible. Avoid watching television or listening to music for at least 15 minutes after returning home and simply enjoy the quietness and tranquillity. This will help to balance your personal energy and make it much easier for you to relax and enjoy the rest of the evening.

Question

I like to use the lounge primarily as a quiet place to relax: to read, listen to music, etc. How can Feng Shui help to create a tranquil atmosphere?

Answer

First of all, ensure that the room is not too bright or too dim. This will make sure that Yin and Yang are balanced and will not cause you to become too unsettled or – at the opposite extreme – drowsy. Once you have done this, pay attention to the plants you have in the room. Because a natural environment is the most perfectly balanced, the more plants you have the better. Balance large plants with smaller ones and ensure that all of them are healthy. Finally, deliberately stimulate the northern zone by placing a crystal, plant or an item containing the colour black in that area. This will promote a greater level of tranquillity throughout the whole room, making your times of relaxation as enjoyable and beneficial as possible.

Question

I often entertain friends informally in the lounge, for coffee, for example. I want to make it feel warm and welcoming, yet encourage lively conversation and shared friendship. Feng Shui principles, please!

Answer

The most important things to consider here are the seating arrangements and the stimulation of the south-western zone, which governs, among other things, general relationships. When seated, you and your friends should be relaxed and comfortable. The seats themselves should not directly oppose each other because this might encourage conflict or arguments. Arrange chairs and sofas so that people sit alongside or at angles with each other. This will allow everyone to communicate openly without the conversaton getting too heated.

The south-western zone should be stimulated with a plant, electrical appliance (a hi-fi would allow you to play background music and stimulate the relationship energy of this zone simultaneously), or the placement of an ornament or picture which contains the colour pink.

Once these steps have been taken, all that will remain is for you to serve coffee and enjoy a warm and lively time together.

4

THE KITCHEN

The kitchen governs the wealth of everyone in your household. The belief behind this is that the kitchen is the place where food is prepared, and food makes family members strong, allowing them to go out into the world and work hard to achieve a higher level of prosperity.

The Ch'i of the kitchen not only affects the person preparing food but everyone in the family, because it affects the prepared food itself. If food is prepared in an environment which is balanced, it will be beneficial to all who eat it. If, on the other hand, food is prepared in an environment which has a lot of negative Ch'i, this negativity will naturally be passed on to anyone who eats it.

The kitchen is therefore a vital part of your home, from both a health and wealth point of view. Creating a perfectly balanced kitchen by applying the principles of Feng Shui will not only help to improve the level of health which you and your family enjoy, but will also have a very good effect on the finances of everyone in your household.

THE DOOR

The door of the kitchen should be free of all obstructions and open as wide as possible to allow Ch'i to enter freely. For this reason you should ensure that the door does not open against a stove or refrigerator, but is allowed to swing freely.

N

NW

NE

W

C

E

SW

SE

S

If the door simply has to open on to an appliance or piece of furniture, hang a crystal on the kitchen side of it so that, as it opens, Ch'i is automatically stimulated. This will help to counter any imbalance caused by a cramped space behind the door.

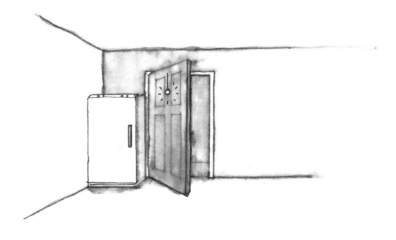

OPEN-PLAN KITCHENS

If your kitchen is open-plan and merges with the dining room or lounge, once again zones of the kitchen may be missing.

In this example the kitchen partly merges with the dining room in the south-eastern zone; this means that the south-eastern Ch'i will be at a lower level than if the kitchen was self-contained. At the same time, the north-eastern Ch'i of the dining room will be at a lower level. The effect of this will be a lack of creativity and wealth in the kitchen and a lack of motivation and purpose in the dining room.

To solve this problem the two rooms should be divided, using a screen, an artificial wall with a second door, or even installing a breakfast bar. If the breakfast bar has a hinged section on the

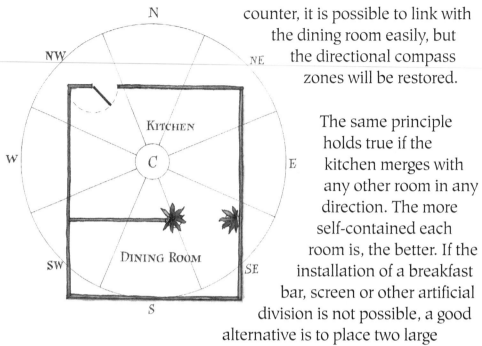

counter, it is possible to link with the dining room easily, but the directional compass zones will be restored.

The same principle holds true if the kitchen merges with any other room in any direction. The more self-contained each room is, the better. If the installation of a breakfast bar, screen or other artificial division is not possible, a good alternative is to place two large plants at the place where the two rooms merge.

This will help stimulate the Ch'i in both the kitchen and the dining room and so counter the effects of having a missing zone in each room.

SERVING HATCHES

Some kitchens are not open-plan as such, but have serving hatches built into a wall so that food can be passed directly into the dining room or lounge. If your kitchen has a serving hatch it is a good idea to fit doors so the hatch can be closed when it is not being

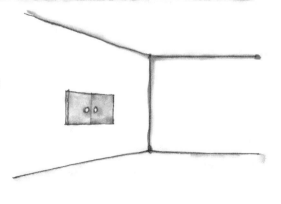

used. Once again, this will help to contain the Ch'i in each room and avoid imbalance.

An alternative to fitting doors is to place a plant inside the hatch itself when it is not in use, so the Ch'i of each room is still contained.

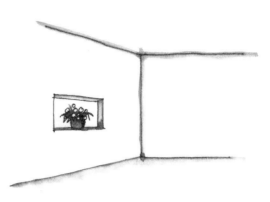

THE STOVE

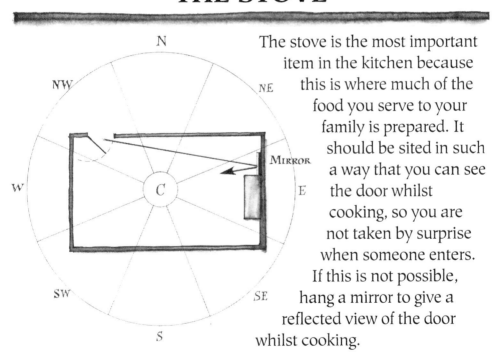

The stove is the most important item in the kitchen because this is where much of the food you serve to your family is prepared. It should be sited in such a way that you can see the door whilst cooking, so you are not taken by surprise when someone enters. If this is not possible, hang a mirror to give a reflected view of the door whilst cooking.

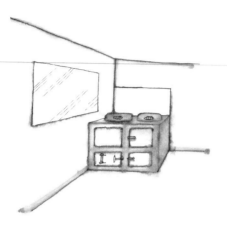

When working at the stove you should not feel cramped or claustrophobic, as this indicates that Ch'i is not flowing smoothly. If you do experience these feelings whilst cooking, perhaps because your stove is in a corner, hang a thin sheet of copper or other reflective metal on the wall to give the illusion of more space. Use reflective metal, because it is resistant to heat.

MICROWAVE

Because most microwave ovens incorporate a digital clock which is running constantly, they are continually drawing from the power supply. This means that you can use your microwave oven to provide electrical stimulation to any zone 24 hours a day, seven days a week.

For example, placing your microwave in the south-western zone of your kitchen would automatically stimulate the surrounding Ch'i, and since this zone governs relationships, tranquillity and practicality, you can expect to experience an improvement in these areas of your life.

If you want to make the most of the metal element which all microwave ovens have, consider placing it in the north-western or western zone, because these are associated with metal; the subsequent Ch'i stimulation will be even more marked.

THE REFRIGERATOR

The refrigerator (and freezer), because it is an electrical item, should be placed in a zone which you particularly want to stimulate. For example, if you want to encourage better family relationships and prosperity, you should place the refrigerator in the western zone. If, on the other hand, you wish to encourage a greater level of tranquillity and practicality, the south-western zone would be more fitting.

The only golden rule you should keep in mind is that the refrigerator should not be placed in the southern zone, because the element of the south is fire and this would conflict with the cool temperature of such equipment.

THE SINK

The positioning of the sink is largely a matter of practicality, unless you are prepared to take on some plumbing work. The ideal position for the sink is in the northern zone, because the element here is that of water. A sink which is regularly used in the north would bring a flowing of water into this zone, and since the north governs tranquillity, sex and career, you can expect these areas of your life to benefit.

If the sink cannot be placed in the ideal northern zone, any of the other zones would be fine, with the exception of the south. As we have just said, the element of the south is fire, and since fire and water do not mix well, this zone is not suitable for a sink.

▶ KITCHEN WITH BREAKFAST BAR

The shape of the breakfast bar in this kitchen is very auspicious, because it is largely octagonal and is therefore symbolic of the Ba-Gua. The only problem with the bar is that the person sitting next to the door may not have a clear view of their neighbour. Placing a small mirror on the wall next to this seat would help to solve this problem.

The placement of dried flowers and other representations of life (such as the cat above the cupboard) is an excellent way to automatically stimulate the flow of Ch'i in the room, and the plant in front of the window ensures that entering solar Ch'i is stimulated directly.

The kitchen is relatively uncluttered, especially in the central area, to allow a free flow of Ch'i, and the yellow colour on the wall is appropriate as the door on that wall leads to the central area of the house.

▶ UNCLUTTERED FAMILY KITCHEN

The oven in this small kitchen is sited in the eastern zone, which is perfect for increasing the levels of health, contentment and optimism of the occupants. Although the oven is set in a corner, lights set above ensure that the Ch'i here is stimulated as much as it possibly could be.

The room is remarkably tidy and uncluttered. The door on the right-hand side of the room is actually a cupboard, and this allows the occupants to store utensils and ingredients in a place where they are easily accessible but will not obstruct the flow of Ch'i.

Thanks to a large window, which provides a pleasant view of the garden, the kitchen is well lit, and correctly leans towards Yang rather than Yin. A plant on the window sill might improve the situation still further.

All in all, this is a kitchen which has been planned well and the occupants will reap appropriate benefits.

◄ **TRADITIONAL-STYLE KITCHEN**

The most striking aspect of this kitchen is the amount of natural light which it receives from the large windows. As the curtains hang outside the window area itself, none of this natural advantage is lost. It ensures that the whole room takes on a healthy Yang quality, and the view of the garden is also extremely beneficial.

The sink is situated in the western zone, so the metal will stimulate the energy governing family prosperity and relationships. The blue washing-up bowl, however, would be better replaced with a white one to take maximum advantage of the beneficial Ch'i in that zone. This is because white belongs to the west, whilst blue is better suited to the north-east. The wooden table is perfectly positioned in the eastern sector.

◄ **KITCHEN/DINING ROOM**

There is a lot of space in this kitchen, and this is accentuated thanks to an open view of the garden and white cupboards. The table, situated in the north-east, is cleverly used to bring the colour blue into the room, and this will give the occupants a greater level of motivation, knowledge and purpose in their lives.

There is good natural lighting, extended by the use of spotlights in the ceiling, and additional lighting under the cupboards where stagnation of energy could occur.

The only question mark from a Feng Shui point of view centres around the positioning of the kitchen trolley. Placed in the middle of an open space it will tend to break up the flow of Ch'i unnecessarily. The flow would be much more even if the trolley were moved towards the side of the room – most profitably in the eastern zone – since this is associated with the element of wood and will help to create greater levels of contentment, optimism and health.

THE WASHING MACHINE

Many Feng Shui practitioners position the washing machine in the northern zone if it is not possible for the sink to be sited there. A washing machine also brings movement of water into the water zone, and because it is an electrical item the Ch'i surrounding it will be stimulated even more.

For the best balance of Ch'i, a washing machine should be as quiet as you can afford. If your washing machine is particularly noisy the sound may disrupt the surrounding Ch'i and cause more harm than good. If a noisy washing machine is placed in the north-west, for example, your ability to lead and plan may be negatively affected. If a noisy machine is placed in the eastern zone, then both your physical and mental health may suffer, typically through higher levels of tension and anxiety.

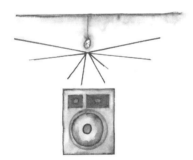

To combat the negative effects of a noisy washing machine you should hang a mobile, small crystal or chime from the ceiling above the machine. This will help to dissipate any negative Ch'i and restore balance to the energy of the kitchen as a whole.

STORAGE SPACE

Storage space is essential in any kitchen, and as far as possible this should take the form of built-in storage units with doors on the front. This is because open shelving in a kitchen can quickly become cluttered and the surrounding Ch'i may then find it difficult to flow smoothly.

If open shelving must be used ensure that it is always tidy and, as far as possible, only use it to store rounded items such as jars, or items of a uniform shape, such as books. If books are

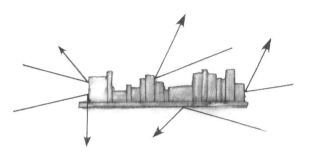

displayed you must also ensure that the spines do not directly face you when cooking. Rows of books, no matter how short, create 'Ch'i daggers' which can, in the long term, be detrimental to your health.

The positioning of closed storage units should be determined solely on the basis of practicality. There is no ideal zone in which items should be stored, and since stored items largely have no effect on

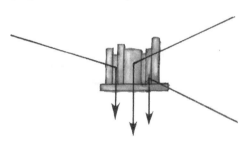

surrounding Ch'i (unless openly stored on shelves, as we have just learned), you have free rein as to where closed storage units are situated.

DECOR

The kitchen should be a place where you feel energetic, optimistic and alive. These are primarily Yang qualities, so angles should feature more prominently than curves and the room should be as light and airy as possible.

When decorating your kitchen aim to strike a balance between the elements of wood and metal. Kitchens which strongly favour metal can feel cold and almost clinical, and the food which is prepared in such a kitchen will lack the warm Ch'i of emotion, making family members more aloof to one another. By the same token, kitchens which strongly favour wood will not feel lively, and food prepared in such a kitchen will make family members feel lethargic and apathetic.

A balanced kitchen which contains approximately the same amount of wood and metal will make the prepared food equally balanced. It will nourish everyone who eats it, making them feel alive and empowered to go out into the world and increase the prosperity and well-being of the entire family.

If you have a lot of metal appliances and surfaces, consider using light, woody colours when decorating the walls, ceiling and floor. Both wall and floor tiles are available in imitation wood and can work quite well when countered by predominantly metal appliances.

If wood already features heavily in your kitchen, adding more metal to the room will be necessary to achieve balance. Consider fitting new metal handles to saucepans and investing in other metal cooking implements which can be hung on the wall when not in use.

Naturally, all surfaces should be kept clean and tidy so that the Ch'i of the kitchen can flow as freely as possible without too much obstruction.

LIGHT

One common problem which many people have with the kitchen is that it feels too cramped. Kitchens are not as expansive as they used to be and this can make them feel dark and claustrophobic. This negatively affects the Ch'i of the room and subsequently of the food which is prepared in it.

You should ensure that as much natural light as possible enters the kitchen, and this is best achieved by using blinds instead of curtains. Blinds can be rolled up during daylight hours and allow solar Ch'i to enter the kitchen very freely indeed, especially when the window is open.

Single or double-paned windows are preferable to windows which have more panes because, generally speaking, the more panes a window has, the more wood or metal there is to block out external light. If possible the glass should be clear rather than frosted, since clear glass does not diffuse the light on impact, whereas frosted glass does.

One final thing to remember is that most people have a tendency to clutter kitchen windows with a variety of trinkets and ornaments, but this clutter also blocks out quite a lot of solar Ch'i. The only thing you should have in front of your window is a plant or a crystal, both of which stimulate the Ch'i as it enters the room.

LIFE (LIVING THINGS)

The best way of bringing life into your kitchen to stimulate the Ch'i of the room, is to cultivate fresh herbs. Mint, parsley, basil, dill and many other herbs can be grown very effectively indoors, and since a lot of herbs have angular, spiky leaves, these will also contribute to a greater level of Yang energy.

Another excellent benefit of cultivating and using fresh herbs in your kitchen is that the Ch'i of the plants will enhance the energy quality of the food you prepare. Food which contains fresh herbs will give anyone who eats it a great spiritual energy boost, making them more passionate about life in general.

Positioning the herbs in your kitchen is much like positioning any other plant. Select the zone you wish to stimulate and place the herbs in that zone to help energise the surrounding Ch'i. For example, if you wish to experience more 'get-up-and-go' in your life, place the herbs in the motivational zone of the north-east. If you would rather enhance your spiritual insight and experience, place them in the tranquillity zone of the north.

If you do not wish to activate any particular zone, herbs can, of course, be placed in front of the window because, being plants, they will automatically energise all solar Ch'i which enters the kitchen in the form of daylight.

MOVEMENT

Hanging a kitchen wall clock is the best way to introduce movement to a kitchen. A metal clock will help to balance an environment which is dominated by wood, and vice versa, but no matter what the clock is made of, it should be hung in a zone which you deliberately want to stimulate.

A pendulum clock in the southern zone of the kitchen will help to increase the amount of energy which you and your family experience. So this would be a good zone if you wish to sustain an active family through the food you serve. A clock in the north-western zone, by comparison, would help to establish greater levels of leadership and responsibility in your home.

ELECTRICITY

Many kitchen appliances are electrical, so there should be no shortage of such items with which you can stimulate the Ch'i of particular zones. Microwaves, blenders, electric kettles and the like all have beneficial effects on the Ch'i surrounding them, so it is perfectly possible to stimulate all eight zones of the kitchen through electricity alone if you spread your appliances around.

Of course, most people are restricted in the positioning of electrical items because of the location of power points. These restrictions can be overcome by using extension leads which are tidily hidden from view or – far preferable – by installing additional power points.

COLOUR

Because the kitchen should primarily be a room where Yang dominates, choose light colours rather than darker ones. Avoid crimsons, dark blues and similar colours and opt for rose whites and lilacs. Plain white, whilst being far too Yang for many rooms, can often be used effectively in a kitchen because it helps to provide a feeling of spaciousness.

If you wish to activate any particular zone in the kitchen by introducing the associated colour, this can be achieved by displaying coloured items. For example, if you want to stimulate the fire Ch'i of the south for a higher social or business profile, you can place a red egg-timer in that zone. If you would rather stimulate the northern Ch'i to help advance the spiritual development of you and your family, you might want to place something black in this zone, such as a mug tree or something similar.

When introducing specific colours into the kitchen once again be sure to avoid placing a colour in the zone of an opposing element. For example, black, being the Feng Shui colour associated with water, should never be placed in the southern fire zone. White and grey, being the colours associated with metal, should never dominate the eastern or south-eastern wood zones.

To sum up ...

Your kitchen governs the health and wealth of your family. Apply these principles of Feng Shui to this important room and you will find that your family becomes more energetic, motivated and prosperous in the outside world.

IMPROVE YOUR LIFESTYLE

How Feng Shui can help you cope with some common problems

Question

Can Feng Shui help encourage teenagers to be less 'faddy' in their eating habits?

Answer

Although there is no specific Feng Shui solution to this problem of dietary awkwardness, many practitioners have found stimulating the eastern zone of the kitchen of great benefit. This may be because faddy eating habits often stem from a lack of contentment. For example, a teenager may decide to eat awkward foods because they feel the need to make a stand or statement about some aspect of life they are unhappy with.

Stimulating the eastern zone with life in the form of fresh green herbs is the best way to encourage a new sense of contentment about life in general, and awkward demands about what foods are acceptable and which aren't should improve considerably. Of course, if the 'faddiness' stems from a genuine principle about life (such as it does with many vegetarians), then nothing will alter this unless a drastic change in principle occurs.

Question

The kitchen seems to be the part of the house where we have 'family conferences' to sort out problems. Can we use Feng Shui to encourage all members of the family to participate positively?

Answer

The answer here is a definite yes. Positive participation will come if the western zone, which governs family relationships, is stimulated effectively. This can be achieved by placing a tray of herbs or an electrical appliance in this area of the room; but remember that an electrical appliance will need to be running if the energy is to be stimulated continuously. A battery- or mains-operated clock would provide the continuous stimulation necessary to promote a good level of participation and strong family relationships.

Question

I always seem to have cash flow problems. Help, please!

Answer

The most important thing you should do when considering your cash flow is to take a close look at how water is flowing in your kitchen, since water represents wealth. If a tap is dripping or water is being wasted for some other reason, this problem should be corrected as soon as possible, as this can cause wealth to be wasted or be in short supply. Once the water in your kitchen flows smoothly, the wealth in your life will tend to follow suit.

Question

I have never been very good at handling money, even though I earn a good salary and am not short of money. Can Feng Shui help?

Answer

Again, you should check to make sure that there are no water leakages in your kitchen, as these will almost certainly cause difficulty in handling money properly. That done, you should take a look at your kitchen from a wider perspective. Spend a few hours ensuring that everything is neat, tidy and well organised – even in cupboards and drawers which are not on view – and then make sure that this level of organisation is maintained. As you do this you will discover that your financial situation also becomes neater, more organised and more manageable.

Question

I am a single parent/divorced/widowed/redundant/a pensioner/ etc. and insufficient money is a constant problem. Can Feng Shui make a difference?

Answer

Certainly. Place a purple ornament or plant in the south-eastern zone. This zone governs wealth, and both the colour purple and life (in the form of a plant) will help to increase the amount of money which flows into your life.

Question

Can Feng Shui strategies encourage a better family atmosphere in the kitchen, encouraging the whole family to share the cooking, washing up and clearing up?

Answer

Yes. You will need to stimulate two zones in particular: the western and south-western zones. The western governs family relationships, and when stimulated your family will quickly get into the habit of becoming considerate to the needs of other members. Stimulating the south-western zone will, in the same way, encourage family members to be more practical, and this will usually show itself in general helpfulness. Both zones can be stimulated through the use of plants, electrical appliances, movement or the placement of crystals.

Question

The kitchen has so many functions in our home, and the children often use the kitchen table for doing their homework. Can we use Feng Shui to encourage a good working atmosphere for them?

Answer

Yes, and in this case it is the north-eastern zone which needs looking at, because this zone governs motivation, knowledge and purpose. Make sure that the zone is stimulated with a plant, crystal or electrical appliance, and if possible encourage the children to work in that corner of the room. The southern zone should be avoided as a homework area because this zone governs passion and energy, and will probably make it very difficult for the children to concentrate for very long. For the same reason you should avoid stimulating the southern zone as much as possible. All this should help encourage productive homework sessions.

Question

I have just started working from home and at present do not have a separate office; the kitchen table is my desk! Suggestions, please, for making the kitchen a purposeful and professional working area.

Answer

If you want to increase income or the profitability of your business, it is a good idea to place a telephone in the south-eastern zone. This will help to ensure that incoming calls are associated with incoming wealth, which usually shows itself in more calls from clients wanting you to work for them. The kitchen should contain a high level of Yang energy, so make sure that there is plenty of natural light in the room and, if the weather permits, open the window to encourage the circulation of more solar Ch'i. Finally, stimulate the northern zone with a plant or crystal, because this will help your career to flourish.

Question

I have just started an Open University/university/college/course, and use the kitchen table to work at home. What Feng Shui strategies should I use to make the atmosphere conducive to clear thinking and application?

Answer

The two zones which are most beneficial to you here are the north-west and north-east. The north-west governs leadership, responsibility and planning, and when stimulated will enable you to apply yourself fully to the task in hand. Stimulation of the north-east will promote greater levels of concentration and clear thinking. I advise you to stimulate the energy in both zones with crystals, since these are highly effective but are small enough to leave plenty of space available for your study notes and reference books.

5

THE DINING ROOM

I n China, the home of Feng Shui, dining is much more than the simple consumption of food. It is a social experience where people communicate with each other and strengthen both their personal and business relationships. When a meal is shared, it symbolises a form of unity between the diners, and when people dine well together their relationships blossom.

Here in the West, too, dining is much more than eating. The most common destination for a first date is a restaurant, because instinctively we know that sharing a meal is, on some level at least, a sharing of ourselves. Meals are at the heart of many of our religious and social celebrations and it is the act of dining with others which make these occasions special.

So it should come as no surprise to learn that your dining room governs your family relationships and communal prosperity. Dining together regularly in a room which adheres to the Feng Shui principles that follow will ensure that you and your family enjoy

► GALLEY KITCHEN

Here we have a long, narrow kitchen which potentially could have negative effects from a Feng Shui point of view. In this case, however, the kitchen is swathed in white and this, in conjunction with the large window, helps to give the room a more spacious, brighter quality.

The room could be made to appear even more spacious if mirrors were positioned on either side of the kitchen – perhaps replacing the blue tiles – but all in all this is a perfect example of how even a small kitchen can be made to appear more bright and spacious through the use of light.

The sink is in a good position in the north of the room, optimising the benefits to tranquillity, sex and career. The oven has a good side view of the door, from where the picture is taken, and the activity of the clock will stimulate good family relationships and general prosperity.

► TRADITIONAL DINING ROOM

This is a very uncluttered room with a wonderful garden view which will make diners feel relaxed and tranquil. The wall light will provide a good level of subtle illumination during the evenings, but the wall itself appears a little too bare. Hanging a mirror on this wall would replace this starkness with a reflected view of the room, giving the impression of opulence and space.

The open bookcase should be moved or fitted with either glass or wooden doors so that Ch'i daggers do not fly in the direction of the diners. Leaving the bookcase where it is without doors could, over the long term, cause the diners to experience digestive problems or possibly worse.

The unit in the left-hand corner of the room serves to display crystal glasses, and this will help to stimulate the Ch'i in this area. However, fitting a light into the unit would increase this stimulation even further, and since the corner lies in the south-eastern zone, this will help the diners to experience more in the way of wealth and creativity.

◄ MODERN DINING ROOM

This dining room has obviously been subjected to some deliberate Feng Shui treatment. Note how a mirror has been carefully positioned to attract more light into the room, and how plants have been placed on either side of the window to stimulate entering solar Ch'i. A few things, however, still need some attention.

The ceiling light shade would benefit from hanging a little lower so that the light bulb itself is not so exposed. In addition, the walls could be brightened if wall lamps were installed, either above or below the pictures which have already been hung. Finally, the dark rug does nothing to contrast with the relatively dark furniture and decor, so this could usefully be replaced with one of a lighter colour. A beige rug, for example, would give the room a lift and make the dining experience more balanced and therefore enjoyable.

◄ INFORMAL DINING ROOM

The natural light which this informal dining room receives is striking. Note how this makes the whole room look fresh and spacious, particularly when diners can enjoy a view of the garden through either the window or the door. The free flow of Ch'i is excellent.

The bowl of fresh fruit on the table will ensure that the surrounding Ch'i is stimulated, and since the dining table is positioned in the north-east, this will make the whole family feel more knowledgeable and motivated. Because the north-east is associated with the colour blue, the curtains in this room are particularly appropriate, as is the crockery – some of which is nicely displayed in the corner unit.

One thing which would improve the room from a Feng Shui point of view is the removal of the rug. Because the table is placed in the north-east, reds and pinks should be avoided wherever possible, since these colours belong to the opposing southern and south-western zones. Beyond that, this is a delightful room which perfectly displays the benefits of having a good level of natural light.

strong, wholesome relationships which are powerful enough to survive almost any negative situation. It will also ensure that every member of your household begins to prosper in all areas of life, including the spiritual, physical, emotional and financial.

THE DOOR

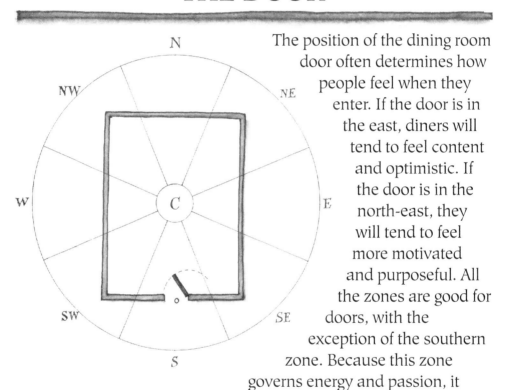

The position of the dining room door often determines how people feel when they enter. If the door is in the east, diners will tend to feel content and optimistic. If the door is in the north-east, they will tend to feel more motivated and purposeful. All the zones are good for doors, with the exception of the southern zone. Because this zone governs energy and passion, it may be difficult for diners entering here to relax during dinner. You can counter this effect by hanging a wind chime or crystal above the door, and by positioning the dining table in the tranquil north; more of this later.

Wherever the door to the dining room is situated in your home, you should ensure that it opens into an expansive area. Doors which open to face a wall (as in the illustration opposite) will make diners feel as though they are imposing, and prevent them from relaxing during the meal. To counter such a situation, hang a mirror or a picture of a distant landscape on the wall so that when the diners enter they are immediately greeted with the illusion of depth.

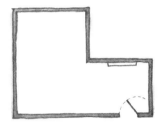

CEILINGS

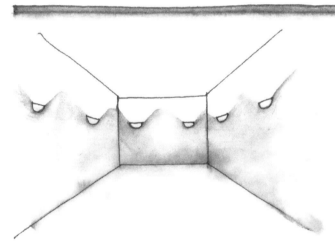

The dining room ceiling should be as high as possible. The golden rule with dining rooms is that the larger they appear the better, because an expansive dining area symbolises wealth for all concerned. If your dining room ceiling is quite low this will drive the Ch'i of the room back down on to the diners quite sharply. This can feel quite oppressive, resulting in a subconscious tendency to rush meals rather then enjoy them at a more relaxed, sociable and productive pace.

To solve the problem of a low dining room ceiling, install wall lights which illuminate the ceiling itself. The additional light on the ceiling will give the impression of greater depth, resulting in a slower moving Ch'i and a more relaxing atmosphere.

OPEN-PLAN DINING ROOMS

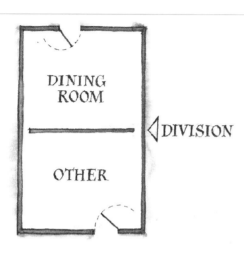

As we discussed when talking about the lounge and the kitchen, open-plan rooms effectively remove one or more of the compass zones from each of the two rooms which merge. If your dining room merges with another room to the east, for example, then the eastern, north-eastern and south-eastern zones will have a much lower level of Ch'i than they would if the room was self-contained.

If you have an open-plan dining room which merges with either the lounge or kitchen, you will already know how to solve this problem. Use a screen, breakfast bar or two fairly large plants to artificially divide the rooms and restore the 'missing' compass points.

THE DINING TABLE

The shape of the dining table should be as simple as possible. Square, rectangular, circular and oval tables are best, and should be as large as your room will allow. A large table symbolises extravagance and abundance, which will make diners feel prosperous before they even begin their meal. A small table, on the other hand, is easily crowded and will make diners feel a little claustrophobic, leading to an imbalance of bodily Ch'i which usually manifests itself as a digestive disorder.

A wooden dining table is far preferable to one made of glass or artificial material, because natural wood radiates a specific Yin energy which is conducive to good dining. If the table is made from one solid piece of wood so much the better, but as long as it has the appearance of being natural and solid even one made from compressed wood shavings (chipboard) is better than a totally artificial alternative.

If the door to your dining room is in the south diners will often be charged with energy, so it is a good idea to place the table in the tranquillity of the northern zone to counter this (see illustration opposite). The positioning of the table in other circumstances depends largely on what you aim to achieve. If you are entertaining business partners, work colleagues or employers on a regular basis, then either the northern or north-

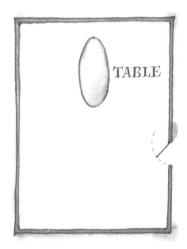

western would be the ideal zones since these govern leadership, responsibility and career progression.

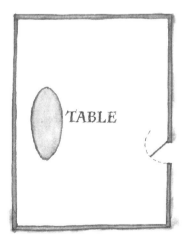

If the majority of your dining is on a more social or family level the western zone would encourage better family relationships (see below); the south-western zone would enhance the quality of your relationships and promote greater levels of peace and tranquillity.

Wherever you site your table the guest of honour should always be seated at the head of the table in such a way that they have a full view of the door. If this is not possible, hang a mirror to give a reflected view of the door. If there is no guest of honour, the head of your household should sit at the head of the table. If equality is important, partners can take it
in turns.

DINING CHAIRS

Because you want your guests or family to be relaxed when dining, excessively angular dining chairs should be avoided. This is because excessive angles are Yang and, as you know, Yang energy makes people more active. At the other extreme, heavily padded or excessively rounded Yin dining chairs may make your diners relax a little too much, and conversation may be slow and unproductive.

A balanced dining chair is one that has both angles and curves, one which allows diners to relax physically yet stay mentally alert. Avoid excessive angles *and* padding and you won't go far wrong!

SOFT FURNISHINGS

Many people enjoy a drink or two before or after dinner, as well as wine with their meal. These can, of course, be drunk in the lounge, but if you have room it is good for the dining room to also have a soft seating area, such as an additional suite, so that guests or family members do not have to wander back and forth.

A dining room suite should be more sturdy than a lounge suite. In this room the intention is not to relax totally, but to remain mentally alert and enjoy one another's company. So pick a more formal and robust suite for this room. Ensure that there are enough seats for everyone and position the seating, once again, according to the benefits you wish to gain.

For example, if you have positioned your dining room table to the north to try and promote career development, a good position for a suite would be in the north-west, since this area governs leadership and responsibility.

Remember, however, if placing an additional suite in the dining room would make the room feel cramped, it is far better to forget the idea altogether. A spacious dining room without a soft seating area is far preferable to one which feels crowded and uncomfortable.

TABLEWARE

The shape of your crockery is just as important as the shape of your table. Again, you should try and use crockery which is simply shaped, but as well as squares, rectangles, ovals and circles, you can also confidently use octagonal plates or dishes. This is because the octagon symbolises the 'Ba-Gua', a particular form of Feng Shui application based on the eight compass directions.

Cutlery can be selected according to personal preference, but should always be well polished so that the metal stimulates the surrounding Ch'i as much as possible.

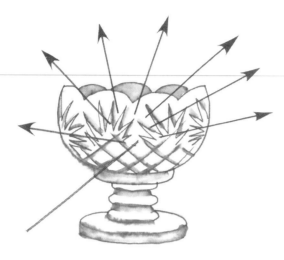

Cut-crystal glasses are excellent at refracting light and stimulating the Ch'i which surrounds them. When filled with clear liquids such as white wine or champagne, they provide each diner with a personal crystal which will have beneficial effects throughout the meal. The glasses do not necessarily have to be expensive to be of benefit, and even cheaper cut glass will stimulate Ch'i through the refraction of light to some extent.

Tablemats should complement the table itself as far as shape is concerned. For example, if you have an oval table then oval tablemats are most suitable so that the Ch'i energy in the dining room flows as smoothly as possible. If the tablemats contain the colour associated with the zone they are used in so much the better, since this will help to stimulate the surrounding Ch'i even more.

For example, if your table is in the western zone and your tablemats contain the colour green, this colour will stimulate the Ch'i of the zone even more, because the west is associated with the colour green. This will result in better family relationships and increased prosperity.

Table linen is also most effective from a Feng Shui perspective if it contains the colour associated with the zone it is used in. Napkins and tablecloths can be obtained in many patterns, but if you prefer white, consider using coloured napkin rings to help stimulate the surrounding Ch'i.

THE FIREPLACE

If your dining room has an open fireplace a fire should be lit at the appropriate time of year when you and your family or guests are using the room. Not only will this give the room a comfortable and 'warm' feel, but the fire itself and the crackling sound it makes will stimulate the surrounding Ch'i very effectively. If a fire is not lit then, as with the lounge, place plants either side of or in the fireplace itself, to stimulate the Ch'i.

The positioning of the dining table is more difficult if there is a fireplace in the room because you should always ensure that diners are not too close to the fire when it is lit. Apart from making sure people are not too hot, this will protect diners from being overwhelmed by the swift movement of Ch'i which a large fire promotes.

DECOR

Because you want your guests to be physically relaxed yet mentally alert whilst dining, the room itself should have a balance of both Yin and Yang energy. You should therefore aim to strike a similar balance between curves and angles and shade and light.

Because the dining table is the most important feature of the room, you should counter its shape in the surrounding decor. For example, if a dining table is square or rectangular, the rest of the decor should be more curvaceous to balance this. This can be achieved with extravagant drapes, a circular dessert trolley and other similarly curved items.

If, on the other hand, the dining table is oval or circular, simpler, more angular shapes should dominate the rest of the room. This can be achieved with a rectangular dessert trolley, sideboard or drinks cabinet, and so on.

LIGHT

Balancing light and shade to achieve equilibrium between Yin and Yang is not the easiest of tasks, but if you aim to illuminate particularly dark corners and avoid the use of excessively strong artificial lights you will not go far wrong. If in doubt, err on the side of Yin or shade, because this relaxes your guests. What you really do not want to do is err on the side of Yang, because this will put your guests on edge and make comfortable conversation difficult to sustain for any length of time.

Dining with one or two candles on the table is an excellent Feng Shui practice because the naked flames will stimulate the Ch'i of the diners but will not make them feel uncomfortable. If you do dine by

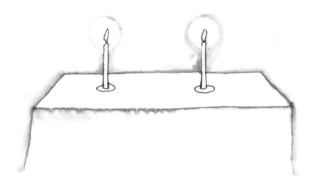

candlelight, however, don't neglect the illumination of the rest of the room. Use table, standard and wall lamps and consider installing a dimmer switch or two, which will allow you to select the exact level of lighting you need quickly and easily.

SOUND

There is often no need for any sound in a dining room as it is hoped that the diners will be more than happy to converse among themselves and thus stimulate the surrounding Ch'i with their own voices. On some occasions, however, it can be beneficial to have some background music. This is especially true when you are dining with people you do not know particularly well, for example, prospective business partners or work colleagues.

Any background music you choose should be gentle and unobtrusive, yet not so quiet that it cannot be heard. The music should be relaxing and help to smooth any pauses in conversation which might otherwise become uncomfortable silences.

So that the background music relaxes all the diners, it should not have lyrics but be acceptable to all tastes. Whilst you may personally enjoy listening both to pop music and Frank Sinatra, many people do not. Most people, however, are happy to hear quiet instrumental music playing in the background because it is subtle and does not challenge their tastes.

As the background music plays, the Ch'i of the room will take on its subtle and relaxing tones and gently lull the bodily Ch'i of each diner into an equally relaxed and joyful state. There is no scope in this book to examine the effect of music on the human Ch'i energy or spirit, but its therapeutic benefits have been cited by many cultures for millennia.

Remember, the golden rule here is to play music which does not intrude on the conversation of the diners, but helps them relax and enjoy each other's company.

MIRRORS

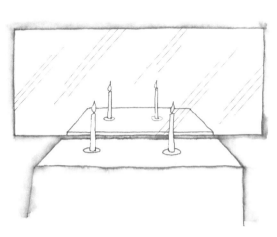

Mirrors can be used to great effect in the dining room. The best use of mirrors is to generate the illusion of space and thus a more extravagant dining area. Hanging a mirror on the wall opposite the dining room table will make the gathering appear twice as impressive and also – because of the way in which Ch'i flows – twice as productive.

Many restaurateurs use mirrors in this way to make their establishments appear larger and more visually extravagant than they really are, and it isn't coincidental that these establishments also appear to be the most popular.

LIFE (LIVING THINGS)

We have already mentioned placing plants in or to each side of a dining room fireplace, but they can also be used as table arrangements. Small arrangements of coloured flowers which co-ordinate with the position of the dining table can help stimulate the Ch'i of the room even further. For example, if your dining table is positioned in the south-western zone, the colour associated with this direction is pink, so pink flowers are most suitable. If, on the other hand, your table is positioned in the eastern zone, then various shades of green would be most suitable because green is the colour associated with this direction.

Because we are aiming for a balance between Yin and Yang, the plants you use should have a mixture of both angular and rounded petals and leaves. Spiky plants should be avoided since these can make diners feel too alert and energetic, making relaxation difficult. Excessively rounded and floppy-leaved plants, on the other hand, can create an atmosphere of lethargy.

As long as it is not positioned in the south, an aquarium which is clean and well-tended will also be beneficial in the dining room. It should not be sited in the south because this direction belongs to the element of fire, and as we have said before, fire and water are not the best of comrades. If the northern zone of the dining room is free, this would be an excellent site for an aquarium, because it belongs to the element of water.

As well as stimulating the Ch'i of the environment through its life, an aquarium can also bring an element of movement into the dining room. Smaller fish which move swiftly through the water will stimulate the surrounding Ch'i much more dramatically than larger, slower fish, so it is a good idea to opt for the former. In a dining room especially, few people want to stare at larger fish because their slow movements may induce a sense of apathy and fatigue. The exception to this rule, of course, is in restaurants, where the larger fish may be on the menu!

ELECTRICITY

Generally speaking, there aren't many electrical appliances in a traditional dining room, but table and standard lamps can be used in conjunction with a mini hi-fi or sound system to stimulate any zones of energy in which you have a particular interest. For example, if you want to stimulate the wealth energy of the south-east, a lamp or hi-fi can be placed here and the desired result will be achieved. By the same token, if you want your family or guests to experience a greater level of self-knowledge and purpose, placing an electrical appliance in the north-eastern zone would accomplish this.

COLOUR

Soft and subtle shades are best suited to the dining room. Once again, you should avoid extremes at all costs so that the colours in the room itself do not intrude on the dining experience.

You can bring specific colours into certain zones to further stimulate the associated Ch'i, for example, by introducing paintings or small soft furnishings into the room. If the dining room window is in the northern zone, for example, and you want to stimulate the career Ch'i by using black, you don't have to (and most people wouldn't want to) hang black curtains. Instead, you could use a black tie to draw the curtains back during daylight hours or keep them together at night.

Always remember that when you are seeking to activate the Ch'i of a particular zone, the quantity of colour is relatively unimportant. A small amount of black will stimulate the Ch'i just as effectively as a pair of solid black curtains. The former, however, will not negatively affect the balance of Yin and Yang in a room, whereas the latter would make the room heavily Yin.

To sum up ...

The dining room is, when all is said and done, the nerve centre of family strength and prosperity. Use the principles discussed in this chapter to both balance and stimulate the energy of this room; the result will be more family satisfaction and prosperity than you have ever experienced before.

► DINING AND SITTING ROOM

This room, which serves as both a sitting room and dining room, is extremely well lit thanks to a large, well-positioned window. The vase of flowers beneath the window serves to attract more solar Ch'i into the room and adds an element of life, ensuring that the energy flow is stimulated as much as possible.

The sofa is well positioned and creates a subtle division between the seating and dining areas, whilst wall lamps in each alcove ensure that potentially dark corners are avoided.

Whilst flowers have been placed above the fireplace, it would be better if a plant was also placed in the fireplace itself when not in use. An empty fireplace can often be prone to a gathering of slow-moving Ch'i, and placing a plant here would help to restore some stimulation.

◄ **BLACK ASH DINING ROOM**

This room features the colour black quite heavily. This will promote greater levels of tranquillity amongst the diners, but is also a marked Yin colour and needs to be balanced with brighter Yang colours. This has been achieved quite nicely through the use of attractive lights and lots of beiges and light browns, although overall the Yin quality is the stronger.

One thing about this dining room which is inauspicious from a Feng Shui point of view is the large number of books on open display. The books point almost directly towards the diners, and could therefore cause them to experience digestive problems or other stomach disorders. For this reason it would be better if the bookcase were moved away from the diners or, preferably, fitted with a glass door to smooth the flow of Ch'i.

The central light provides good overall lighting, but perhaps some additional wall or table lights would give more control over the levels of lighting to suit particular moods.

◄ **COLOURFUL BEDROOM**

The colours in this bedroom lean correctly towards Yin rather than Yang, creating a relaxing environment which is ideal for rest and sleep. However, the head of the bed is positioned in the southern zone, and whilst this will promote a more passionate sex life, it can also make sleep quite difficult. The positions of the wardrobes and the bed could therefore be reversed so that the head of the bed is in the northern zone and the wardrobe in the south.

The family pictures in the room provide a nice personal touch, but concentrating a large number of photographs in one area is not necessarily the best arrangement. It would be better to spread the pictures more evenly around the room so that the resultant Ch'i flow is also more even and smooth.

IMPROVE YOUR LIFESTYLE

How Feng Shui can help you cope with some common problems

Question

Everyone seems to be so rushed these days that there's little time to enjoy quality time together. How can we use Feng Shui to encourage the whole family to sit down to eat and talk together properly in the dining room?

Answer

The key here is to prepare the room so that Yin outweighs Yang. Yin, which is associated with inactivity, will cause everyone in the room to relax more than they otherwise might. This can be achieved by ensuring that the dining room is not too brightly lit, and that furnishings are curved rather than angled. Couple this with deliberate stimulation of the western zone which governs family relationships (through the placement of a plant, crystal or white object) and the result should be a much more relaxed dining atmosphere in which the individual family members can enjoy each other's company and engage in stimulating and interesting conversation.

Question

I have to cater for both an elderly relative with a very poor appetite and for difficult teenagers with faddy eating habits. Can Feng Shui help in either case?

Answer

Problems with diet can often be alleviated through the use of Feng Shui. Stimulation of the eastern zone usually works best, as it is this zone which governs both contentment and health, and when people are happy and content and feel healthy and well they tend to enjoy a healthy amount and range of food. Because green is the colour associated with the east, the best way to stimulate the energy in this zone is to place a large, round-leafed plant in this area.

Question

We frequently entertain guests in our home. When we give lunch or supper parties we want to make our guests feel welcome and relaxed. How can Feng Shui help?

Answer

Subconsciously, the first thing people notice when they enter any room is any imbalance between Yin and Yang and any disruption in the flow of Ch'i in the room. Both of these will make guests uncomfortable, although in the majority of cases they will not know why they feel like this.

The best way to make your guests feel both welcome and relaxed is to ensure that the dining room is neither excessively bright nor dim, thus balancing Yin and Yang. Having done that, you might consider hanging a decorative mobile or small chandelier in the centre of the room to help keep the Ch'i of the room flowing in a smooth, even manner. Play some gentle, soothing music quietly in the background and your guests will quickly settle in and feel relaxed and sociable, resulting in an enjoyable meal for all concerned.

Question

I love having guests for dinner parties, but I find being a host/ hostess quite stressful. Can I use Feng Shui to help me to be an effective host/hostess – and to help me relax and enjoy the company of my friends and colleagues?

Answer

What you must try to do is prepare the atmosphere not only for your guests, but also for yourself as you set about arranging the meal. Ensure that you allow plenty of time to prepare the meal and dining room, as rushing will charge you with Yang energy and make later relaxation more difficult. Also, try to enjoy the actual preparation of the meal. Make sure you have plenty of time, play tranquil music in the background as you work, avoid excessively bright artificial lighting and stimulate the south-western zone with a small crystal. The stimulation of this zone will not only give you a sense of tranquillity and happiness as you work, but it will also help you to enjoy the development of your friendship with your guests when they arrive.

Question

Conversation at dinner parties can often be stilted and formal. Can Feng Shui help to encourage lively, friendly conversation when people come for a meal, particularly when the guests are meeting for the first time?

Answer

Again, it is the south-western zone which needs particular stimulation in this case. Guests meeting for the first time can often be nervous and perhaps even anxious, and so will benefit from the tranquillity associated with this area. Having a pink-flowered potted plant in this zone will provide the necessary stimulation very effectively, because the south-western zone is associated with the colour pink and the earth element, but do make sure that the plant is in flower!

Question

I've recently been made redundant/taken early retirement and am setting up a business from home, so the dining room is currently doubling as my office. How can I use Feng Shui to create a productive working atmosphere?

Answer

To start with, you should make sure you work in the south-eastern zone of the room, as this governs wealth and creativity. Since this zone is associated with the element of wood, if you are using a wooden dining table as a desk this will also help to speed up the development of your new business.

As far as productivity is concerned, the greater the amount of natural light in the room, the better. You should also open a window if the weather allows, so that a constant circulation of Yang energy can be experienced. This will give you much more personal energy and vitality to tackle projects effectively. If you need to spend a lot of time thinking about your business goals and making plans, you should do this in the north-western zone if at all possible, since this zone governs leadership, responsibility and planning, and will help you to clarify and organise your thoughts logically and effectively.

Question

I've just enrolled at college as a mature student after many years away from study, and use the dining room to work in during the day and at weekends. Can I employ Feng Shui principles to create a stimulating atmosphere for study? I know I shall find it hard to get my brain into gear again!

Answer

What you need to do in this situation is stimulate the north-eastern zone of the room, which is associated with motivation, knowledge and purpose. Having a blue-flowered pot plant here will do the job very nicely, because both the colour blue and the element earth belong to this compass point. Your last comment suggests that the amount of personal 'get up and go' you feel you need may be lacking. If you need to generate more passion and energy for your studies, you should light a red candle in the southern zone, but if you become too restless extinguish the candle, as it is possible that the red may distract you.

Taking these measures should ensure that your studies are as fruitful and enjoyable as possible.

6

THE BEDROOMS

We spend a third of our lives asleep, and if we take 'three score years and ten' as the average life-span of a human being, this equates to us spending over 23 years in bed, or four months each year. This fact alone makes the bedroom very important, because Ch'i affects us whether we are conscious of it or not.

If we spend these four months each year sleeping in a bedroom where Ch'i is not flowing correctly, our bodily Ch'i will suffer as a result and this can lead to any number of health problems. Poor Ch'i circulation can manifest itself as anything from nightmares and insomnia to more serious conditions such as depression.

The bedroom, as well as being the place where we sleep and recharge our physical energy, is also a very personal refuge. It is the place where we most commonly enjoy sexual relationships and feel truly liberated and free to do whatever we like.

By applying the principles of Feng Shui to the bedrooms in your home the lives of you and your family can be improved quite dramatically. Children can experience a greater sense of well-being and security. Adults can enjoy better sex lives and more direction in their business and social lives. Adolescents can achieve a higher level of success in academic studies and examinations.

THE DOOR

MIRROR

The entrance to a bedroom should not be obstructed in any way. The Ch'i of the home should be free to flow straight into the room without being disturbed by immediate pieces of furniture such as dressers or bedside cabinets. If a bedroom is so small that some obstruction simply cannot be avoided (quite common in children's rooms), a small mirror should be hung so that the illusion of greater depth is created.

THE BED

Without doubt the most important piece of furniture in the bedroom is the bed itself. If the Ch'i energy is to flow in a perfectly balanced manner it stands to reason that the bed, being the dominant bedroom item, must help rather than hinder the flow.

There are a wide variety of beds available, but the golden rule is to aim for simplicity. Preference should be given to beds 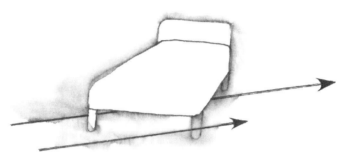 which appear smooth to the eye, with rounded edges that help the Ch'i glide over them without effort.

Excessively angled beds, such as four-posters, can disrupt this smooth flow of energy and create sharp currents which may eventually become harmful. Note how the square legs on the bed illustrated below obstruct the Ch'i quite significantly.

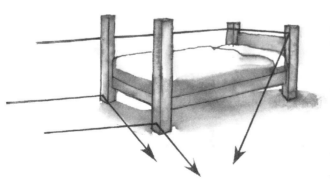 If you really have no choice but to use a bed which has an excess of angles, you will need to tone down these angles as much as possible. A valance is often useful to disguise lower angles such as square legs. Try to visualise the current of energy flowing over the bed; if the valance helps to smooth out most of the

sharp edges, it has done its job. Dressing the top of a four-poster bed with complementary drapes will achieve a similar result.

The headboard of the bed should also be as unobtrusive as possible. Most modern headboards are naturally curved, so this will not be a problem in the majority of households, but if you have one which is excessively angular then you risk disrupting the flow of Ch'i. This may result in sleeplessness, which will naturally lead to irritability and possibly even a deterioration in personal relationships.

POSITIONING THE BED

The positioning of the bed should be determined by the ambitions or desires of the sleeper. If you want a more satisfying sex life, for example, the head of the bed should be positioned to the north, because the northern zone governs sex. If you enjoy your sex life but would like your love-making to be more passionate, you could place the head of your bed in the south, whose energy governs passion. If you take this latter option, however, you should be prepared for quite a few sleepless nights, because this zone also increases the amount of energy you will experience.

If you would like to improve your financial prosperity, positioning the head of the bed in the south-eastern zone will help you to accomplish this. In the same way, positioning the head of the bed in the western zone will help you experience better family relationships and communal prosperity.

The positioning of a bed in a child's room should be thought about carefully and based on what you want your child to experience. If your child has low self-esteem and is of a nervous disposition, placing the head of the bed in the eastern zone will encourage

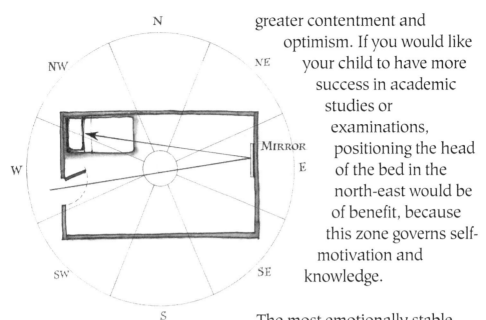

greater contentment and optimism. If you would like your child to have more success in academic studies or examinations, positioning the head of the bed in the north-east would be of benefit, because this zone governs self-motivation and knowledge.

The most emotionally stable zone for a child who sometimes feels insecure and is prone to nightmares is the spiritual zone of the north. Placing the head of the bed here will bathe your child in the Ch'i of tranquillity and encourage a good night's sleep.

Once you have positioned your bed, lie down and make sure you have a clear view of the bedroom door. This is because if people enter the bedroom by surprise it can disrupt the flow of Ch'i and cause the sleeper to feel restless and uncomfortable, and this in turn will make it difficult to get to sleep.

If the door cannot be seen from the bed you should use a mirror to give you the necessary view. The illustration below shows the position of a bed for someone who desires success in forthcoming academic examinations, but cannot see the door clearly from the appropriate position, and has therefore used a mirror.

THE WARDROBE

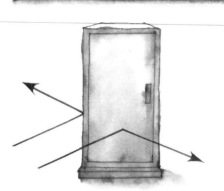

If your wardrobes are built into a wall of the room there is usually no need to move them because they will act like the wall itself. If wardrobes are free-standing, however, they can obstruct the Ch'i of the room because they tend to be boxy and angular.

To make a wardrobe less obstructive hang a full-length mirror on the door and a small mirror on each side. This will effectively 'cancel out' any obstruction which the wardrobe causes and will help the surrounding Ch'i energy to flow much more smoothly.

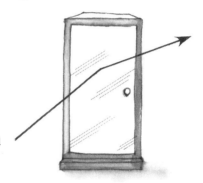

BEDSIDE TABLES AND CABINETS

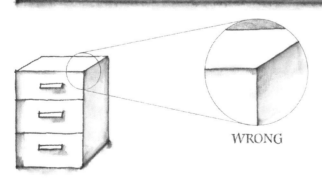

WRONG

Because the bedroom is a place primarily intended for sleeping, there should be as few angles as possible next to the bed itself. Angular bedside tables and cabinets should therefore be avoided if at all possible and preference given to ones which are more curved. Square and rectangular cabinets are acceptable if the wood is curved at the edges. What you don't want are sharp, precise corners and angles.

The bedside table or cabinet should not stand higher than the top of the mattress when placed beside the bed because this will stop the Ch'i of the room from circulating freely over

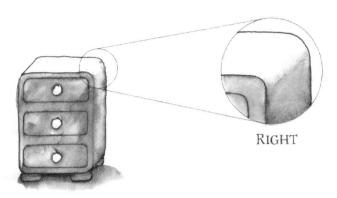

RIGHT

your head whilst you are sleeping. This can cause you to wake with headaches or even prevent you from sleeping.

THE DRESSING TABLE

First of all, you should ensure that the mirror on your dressing table is as large as possible, since this can help to make the whole bedroom look that much larger and brighter. Again aim for curves rather than angles, so that the Ch'i energy of the room flows as smoothly as possible.

Positioning the dressing table depends largely on the structure of your bedroom and personal taste. Because its focal point is the mirror, a dressing table can be placed in any zone without adverse effects. Having said that, it is usually most beneficial to place it in a zone which normally looks dark and claustrophobic, such as in a poorly lit corner. Here the mirror will attract extra light and make the corner appear more spacious than it really is.

BEDROOM CHAIRS

Comfort and practicality are the key words here, and as long as the chair(s) has rounded, smooth surfaces, personal taste should be exercised. Positioning the chair is, once again, largely a matter of your own preference, but if you tend to hang clothes, etc. on a chair, it should not be placed next to the bed. Clutter next to the bed – even if it is just a few clothes – can cause disruption to sleep patterns and even cause inferior health in the long term.

DECOR

The bedroom should, generally speaking, lean further towards Yin than Yang, so you should try to choose curves over angles and avoid excessively bright artificial lighting.

Decorating the bedroom is largely a matter of personal taste and should reflect the passions of the individual, but be aware that large amounts of black on the walls could cause depression in some people. For adults, soft, subtle colours are usually the best because these will give you a pleasant lift in the morning but will not keep you awake at night. For children, brighter colours can be introduced against a subtly coloured background in the form of posters, curtains and duvet sets with motifs, as long as these motifs are acceptable and enjoyed by the child.

The floor of any bedroom should be carpeted, and the rule here is that the thicker the pile of the carpet the better. Soft, thick fabrics are primarily Yin and are very relaxing, which makes them ideally suited to bedrooms.

Curtains and/or blinds should be as thick as necessary to block out external light whenever necessary. Soft, luxurious fabrics are preferred, since these are primarily Yin and will help ensure that you get the maximum possible benefit from sleep. You should also consider having curtains or blinds which contain the colour associated with the zone they are to be used in, unless your window is in the south. Placing red in the south will stimulate the Ch'i associated with energy and can cause sleeplessness.

LIGHT

In the daytime, you want to encourage as much natural light as possible into the bedroom so that the room receives a good in-flow of solar Ch'i.

At night, however, natural light may need to be blocked so that sleep is possible. This is especially true in a child's bedroom or that of an adult who works shifts. People who go to bed in the early evening might find it difficult to sleep in the summer months because of 'excessive' daylight bringing too much Yang energy into the room.

To solve this problem, first ensure that the bed is not placed directly beneath the window, then consider fitting a dark blind to the bedroom window instead of curtains. In the daytime the blind can be rolled up to allow the beneficial Ch'i of the sun to flow into the room, but when you want to sleep it can be rolled down and this will block out much of the light and decrease the level of Yang energy.

Artificial lighting should be simple. Installing a dimmer switch will enable you to set the level of lighting to one that is most suited to your requirements, but if this is not possible use bedside lamps and wall-mounted light fittings which are aimed towards the ceiling.

► SPACIOUS BEDROOM

This is quite a spacious room, but a little lacking in colour. This could be solved by using a more colourful duvet cover and/or replacing the existing pictures with larger, more detailed ones. The colours selected should relate to the overall position of the room in the house; or they should aim to stimulate the relevant area of the room.

The head of the bed is positioned in the northern zone, and this will help the occupants to get the most from their sleep. Having a television in the room however, may be something of a distraction – especially since it is so prominently positioned – but this is a matter of personal choice.

The subtle lights above the bed and on the wall help to ensure that the room does not lean too far towards Yang in the evenings, but if sleeping becomes a problem then perhaps bedside lights should replace those directly above the pillows.

► BEDROOM WITH CANOPIES AND FITTED WARDROBES

This bedroom leans towards Yang in that there are more angles than curves and the duvet colours are perhaps a little too vibrant to be conducive to a good night's sleep. One major problem is that the canopies over each bed form striking angles. These may well cause sleeplessness and maybe even headaches, so a more curvaceous, flowing arrangement should be considered, using a little more fabric or draping it in such a way to create curves. The same problem exists with the headboards, which are rather angular and would be better replaced with half-moon shapes and padded with soft fabrics.

The use of artificial lighting is good, but in the summer sleeplessness may be caused by an excess of natural light entering the room directly opposite the beds. To solve this potential problem, darker curtains could be hung so that the occupants have the option of blocking out as much solar Ch'i as possible throughout the evenings.

◄ **BEDROOM WITH FITTED FURNITURE AND MIRRORS**

Again, this bedroom leans rather heavily towards Yang. There is a tremendous amount of light in this room, accentuated by the extensive use of mirrors. Some are visible here in the corner of the room, but more mirror-faced cupboards are positioned to the left of the door, from which the photograph is taken. This excess of light needs tempering if sleep is to be as beneficial as possible. Dark, heavy curtains could be hung to block out natural light when necessary.

The bed is positioned under some harsh angles, but since these are part of the fitted bedroom and cannot easily be moved, a small crystal should be placed on the shelf above the bed to smooth the flow of Ch'i.

A large plant is also positioned by the door, and this is an excellent feature as it stimulates the Ch'i in what otherwise could be quite a stagnant corner. The plant will also help to keep the air in the room fresh and alive, and this will contribute to more productive sleep.

◄ **OPEN-PLAN LIVING ROOM**

This is not the easiest of rooms to deal with as far as Feng Shui is concerned because of its unusual shape, but the occupants have done remarkably well. An artificial division between the dining and lounge areas has been created with the use of a central bar, and any straying Ch'i is stimulated by the large plant which has been placed by this division and also by the basket of fruit which has been placed on the bar itself.

Both the dining and lounge areas benefit from a good level of natural light, but the chair in front of the window in the lounge should be moved to avoid obstructing this solar Ch'i.

In the dining area, the books on display would benefit from being moved so that the Ch'i daggers do not affect the bodily Ch'i of the diners. Similarly, books should not be allowed to accumulate on the black shelving unit. Beyond that, this room proves that even the most awkwardly shaped room can benefit from the deliberate use of Feng Shui principles.

Sleeping under a light fitting which hangs from the ceiling can cause headaches, so this is not recommended. If a ceiling light must be positioned above the bed, use a light shade which corresponds to the zone it lies in. For example, if a ceiling light is in the south-western zone, a pink light shade will be most suitable. By using a light shade of the corresponding zone colour, the light will stimulate the surrounding Ch'i when in use; this can counter any negative effects that sleeping under the light fitting may have.

SOUND

In the main, the less sound in the bedroom, the better. This is simply because sleep comes more easily in silence than if there is noise or music playing in the background. Hanging a chime in the bedroom is not recommended because it can disturb sleep, and in the long term disturbed sleep will negatively affect your temperament and emotions.

Alarm clocks are very popular and most people use them, but you should pay attention to the kind of noise your alarm clock emits. Waking up to a shrieking buzzer or whistle will immediately disturb the balance of your bodily Ch'i. This is why such alarms often make you leap out of bed without thinking, whenever they go off.

If you want to wake up on time but still keep your bodily Ch'i in balance, invest in a radio alarm clock and select a station which plays a lot of classical music. Do not set the volume too high, but ensure that the radio will be audible when it switches itself on at the appropriate time. Doing this will ensure that you wake to a sound which soothes your bodily Ch'i, so the rest of your day will be all the more peaceful and enjoyable.

LIFE (LIVING THINGS)

Plants not only stimulate the Ch'i of the room, but also improve the quality of the air and make sleeping even more beneficial than usual. Plants used in the bedroom should have large, rounded leaves because these are associated with Yin energy and have a relaxing effect on everyone in the room.

You should position your plants in zones which you particularly want to stimulate. If you want to experience a more adventurous and passionate sex life without moving your bed into the southern zone, a plant can be placed there instead. If you find that activating this zone makes sleeping difficult (because, as we said earlier, it also governs energy), you can simply move the plant to another area.

MOVEMENT

The best way of introducing movement into a bedroom is by using a mobile. Once mobiles were aimed solely at children, but many manufacturers are now producing decorative mobiles for adult rooms too.

A mobile will sway in even the lightest breeze and this movement will stimulate the Ch'i which surrounds it. If you want to improve your creativity, hanging a mobile in the corresponding south-eastern zone will help you accomplish this. By the same token, hanging a mobile in the northern zone will help you develop greater levels of spiritual awareness, and so on.

ELECTRICITY

The bedroom is not the most obvious place for electrical items, but most people have an electrical alarm clock or bedside lamp and these can be positioned – as you will be well aware of by now – in any zone which you particularly want to stimulate.

Many people now have a television set in their bedroom, but on the whole I would not recommend this if you share your bedroom with a partner, as it can quickly make the quality of communication and your relationship deteriorate if it is used on a regular basis. The only time I would personally allow a television set in a bedroom is when an individual sleeps alone and does not have to worry about such a deterioration.

COLOUR

Bringing out the energy of any given zone by using colour is far easier in a bedroom than anywhere else. Ornaments, posters, paintings, fluffy toys and all manner of other items can be used, according to your personal tastes, to stimulate the Ch'i with specific colours.

For example, a drama student who wishes to become a famous actor or actress could place something red in the southern part of the room. This would help them because this zone governs the social and public profile of an individual. At the same time a student could place a painting or other item which features the colour purple in the south-eastern zone, since this area governs creativity and would help them develop their performance.

To sum up ...

By now you will have realised that Feng Shui is a very flexible science which allows you to use its principles without infringing on your personal taste or sense of style. This is truer in the bedroom than in any other room, because the bedroom is truly a place that you can call your own, where you do not have to worry too much about the opinions and tastes of other people.

Applying the principles of Feng Shui to your bedroom and those of your family will ensure that the time you spend there, and particularly your sleep, is as beneficial as possible, and that the third of your life spent sleeping is positively enhanced.

IMPROVE YOUR LIFESTYLE

How Feng Shui can help you cope with some common problems

Question

My children find it very difficult to get to sleep, particularly in the summer, and often wake during the night. Feng Shui suggestions, please!

Answer

The problem here is almost certainly due to the amount of solar Ch'i in the room. During the summer our rooms are flooded with solar Ch'i, and the Yang quality of the energy escalates dramatically. Since the days are long
in the summer months, the energy of the room does not become truly balanced with Yin until the early hours of the morning, and so sleeplessness is the result.

To solve this, close the curtains in the bedroom a few hours before it is time for your children to go to bed, and unless humidity is likely to be a problem, make sure that the windows are closed too. This will reduce the amount of solar Ch'i entering the room and the Yin created through darkness will balance the energy much faster, leading to better sleeping conditions for all concerned.

Question

Until recently, I was always a good, heavy sleeper. However, now I am menopausal/elderly I find I am becoming increasingly insomniac! Can I use Feng Shui to get a good night's sleep?

Answer

Placing your bed in the northern zone is essential for most insomniacs, since this is the zone which governs tranquillity and is the most conducive to sleep. At the same time, you should ensure that the southern zone is being stimulated as little as possible by introducing something black into that area. Black is the colour associated with the water element, and so will reduce the amount of energy which the southern zone is creating.

You should also make sure that the room is always as dark as possible so that Yin dominates. A dimmer switch is very effective in ensuring that the room is never lit more than it need be, and all of this taken together should provide you with sound sleep.

Question

I work different hours each week, with some night work involved, which is playing havoc with my sleep patterns. Can Feng Shui help me sleep during daylight hours and work at night?

Answer

This is another question of Yin and Yang. Working at night when Yin prevails is not entirely natural. By the same token, neither is sleeping during the day when Yang is abundant. What you must try to do is ensure that your place of work is as brightly lit as possible, and at the same time take any measures necessary to block out light from your bedroom when you are sleeping. This will 'trick' your bodily Ch'i into treating night as day, and vice versa.

Once again, sleeping in the north will be beneficial, and any stimulation of the southern zone should be reduced through the placement of a black item in that area.

Question

*I am finding that sleeplessness is a problem since a bereavement/
divorce/redundancy/etc. Can Feng Shui principles help to promote
better sleep patterns?*

Answer

Sleeplessness is a real problem for many people and for many
different reasons. Bereavement, divorce and redundancy are
examples of situations in which our bodily Ch'i suffers heavy
disruption caused by very volatile emotions. Fortunately, Feng Shui
can help to promote better sleep in all these circumstances. The
solution is to stimulate the northern zone and avoid stimulating the
southern. Follow the advice I gave earlier in this section regarding
insomnia and the results should be the same: a balancing of bodily
Ch'i and a leaning towards Yin, both of which are necessary for a
good night's sleep.

Question

*We live in a very noisy neighbourhood, which constantly affects
our ability to get to sleep and frequently wakes us in the night.
Suggestions, please.*

Answer

Unlike light, noise is something which is very difficult to block out of
our homes – even using Feng Shui principles. You should consider
installing double glazing if you do not already have it, but apart from
that your only course of action is to follow the instructions given
earlier in this section for combating insomnia.

Question

Our sex life is comfortable but unexciting. Can Feng Shui help?

Answer

Feng Shui can certainly help to spice up your sex life, but the price for this will probably be at least a few sleepless nights! Seriously, putting the excitement back into your sex life is simply a matter of stimulating the southern zone of your bedroom as much as possible. Move your bed to the southern zone and stimulate the energy of this area by using the colour red as much as possible. Buy some red satin sheets and wear red lingerie. A red bulb in a bedside lamp has been found by many couples to spark sexual miracles, but this is not to the taste of everyone.

In a nutshell, as long as the southern zone contains both bed and red, you can expect an almost instant increase in passion and sexual adventure.

Question

We are newly married/just setting out on a new partnership/ and want to ensure that our sexual and emotional relationship is as good and enduring as possible. How can Feng Shui help?

Answer

As you rightly suggest, both sexual and emotional satisfaction is vital to any long-lasting relationship. The northern zone governs sex and tranquillity, and in the main sleeping in this area and deliberately stimulating it by placing a black object or crystal above the bed will provide the balance you are looking for. Occasionally, however, you should move your bed to the southern zone and follow the instructions given in the last answer so that your relationship does not become stale and boring. You should also remember that although Feng Shui is extremely effective, it can never replace the benefit of good communication and conversation between you and your partner.

Question

Our 10-year-old marriage/partnership seems to have reached an emotional and sexual impasse. How can we 'unblock' the relationship and move forward again?

Answer

The emotional quality of a relationship can, in normal circumstances, only be as good as the quality of the sex life, and vice versa. This means that to unblock your 'impasse' you will need to stimulate two zones: the south to restore passion to the sexual side of your relationship, and the west to improve the emotional side.

To stimulate the southern zone, follow the instructions given earlier for solving a 'comfortable but unexciting' sex life. To stimulate the western zone, place a white metal object (both white and metal being associated with the west) in this area. This could take the form of an ornament, radio or alarm clock.

Doing this should result in an 'unblocking' of your relationship and should ensure that it is satisfying and productive from both an emotional and sexual point of view.

Question

The children do their homework in their bedrooms. How can we use Feng Shui to create an effective working atmosphere for them, bearing in mind that their bedrooms are also their 'bolt holes' and their place to 'chill out'?

Answer

The key here is to try and get your children involved in the re-arrangement of their bedrooms as they think of them as their personal territories and may resent interference in the layout. The promise of a new desk or other study-related 'reward' will help to get them on-side and assist you in applying Feng Shui techniques to the room. As far as particular principles are concerned, there is only so much a parent can do without encroaching on the 'personal space' of a child. Arranging the room so that study is done in the north-east is probably the most important thing you can do, and if the colour blue occupies this space then so much the better.

Another strategy would be to speak to your child about Feng Shui and treat the whole thing as a 'game' which could help them make their homework less of a chore. The possibility of eradicating a 'chore' or making it easier will often be all it takes to get full co-operation from your child.

Question

The noise coming from our adolescent children's bedrooms – loud music/radio/friends coming round/etc. – disrupts the rest of the household. Could Feng Shui help make them a little more aware of other people?

Answer

Again, this depends largely on how co-operative your children are. If co-operation is non-existent, perhaps the best thing you can do is buy them a gift which can be placed in the western zone of their bedrooms to stimulate the energy associated with family relationships. For example, a white bedroom clock hung on the western wall will stimulate the Ch'i of this area, and if the clock has a sweeping second hand, this movement will stimulate the energy even more.

If your children are more co-operative, make sure they are aware of the disruption which is sometimes caused and offer to help set new ground rules which will benefit everyone. Often, if children are treated as adults and feel 'grown up' they will be more adult in their behaviour and this may well solve the problem.

Question

My bedroom is not just where I sleep; it's my 'eyrie', a quiet place where I relax and recharge my batteries, reading, listening to music or the radio in bed. How can I use Feng Shui to give it a very tranquil atmosphere?

Answer

Tranquillity is governed by the northern zone, so aim to stimulate the north with the colour black and perhaps also the introduction of water. A small aquarium or fish bowl in the north will provide movement and stimulate the surrounding Ch'i very well. Consider hanging a picture containing some black on the northern wall, as this will also bring out the tranquillity of the room.

Finally, be sure to avoid stimulating the southern zone, since this wall will destroy any tranquillity you might otherwise experience. Keep reds in this zone to a minimum if at all possible.

Question

I often go to bed to work: to write work reports; plan out my university/Open University/college/school/ essays; read the minutes of meetings I've got to attend; write that novel which will make me famous one day, and so on. So I want my bedroom to be relaxing, but not too much so. Feng Shui strategies, please!

Answer

Your question indicates that the energy you really need is that of creativity. To achieve this I suggest you move your bed into the south-eastern zone and stimulate the energy with a bedside or wall lamp which contains the colour purple.

7

THE BATHROOM

Money has been associated with water for centuries. We refer to money as 'flowing' in and out of our lives. We talk of people who, because of their extravagant spending habits, are said to 'spend money like water'. We even talk about money being 'in circulation' as though it is a liquid pool which never stands still. Feng Shui is no different, and because the bathroom is one in which water flows on a regular basis, it is said to govern the wealth and financial prosperity of the entire household.

Unfortunately, many people consider the bathroom to be one of the least important rooms, and so tend to concentrate much more on the appearance and layout of communal areas such as the lounge or dining room. If you give the bathroom the attention it deserves, however, and apply the principles of Feng Shui as fully as you can, you may experience a very welcome transformation in your financial status in a surprisingly short space of time.

▶ CHILDREN'S BEDROOM

Keeping the centre of a room of one or more children free of clutter can be tremendously difficult, but in this case it has been achieved by storing the majority of toys underneath the window. Strong, vibrant colours lean towards Yang, but children will feel more comfortable in favourite duvets, so this is not too much of a problem.

One thing which would benefit from attention is the picture which hangs above the top bunk bed. Not only is the picture angular, but the cord which it hangs from also forms a sharp angle, and neither of these factors will help to encourage sleep. Removing the picture or replacing it with an oval or circular-shaped one would be the best solution.

As far as bunk beds go, they are often necessary evils. The sharp angles formed by many bunk beds can result in restlessness and hyperactivity in small children, but in this case care has been taken to ensure that the edges of the bed are as rounded as possible.

The choice of light shade is a good one because it serves not only to avoid flooding the room with light, but also to bring a curved element into play.

This is a good example of how Feng Shui principles can be used even in the rooms of small children – often the most difficult bedrooms of all.

▶ SMALL HALLWAY

Despite this being quite a small hallway, this is an excellent example of how keeping a hall free of clutter can give a good impression of space and allow the Ch'i to flow smoothly. A mirror has been hung in the area near the bottom of the stairs to keep the speed of the energy flow in check, whilst the whole area benefits from a good amount of natural light thanks to the plain glass door.

Because the door of the hall has been held back, visitors to this home will be greeted by a welcoming open space. This will serve to make them feel relaxed and ensure that subsequent relationships start as well as possible.

◄ COLOURFUL WIDE HALLWAY

This is a perfect example of a moderately wide hallway. Dragons, which are very auspicious creatures from a Feng Shui perspective, are positioned above the main door. This will bless everyone who enters and leaves the home via this door, yet the dragons themselves are quite unobtrusive and do not immediately draw attention to themselves.

The decorative window in the door itself represents a good balance of Yin and Yang, since it mixes angles and curves and a variety of colours in an even, attractive manner.

Finally, having the hall free from clutter will ensure that visitors feel relaxed and comfortable as soon as they enter.

◄ HALLWAY WITH OAK STAIRCASE

This porch and hallway shows how even the most complicated entrance to a home can appear simple if the space is kept free of clutter. The porch is well lit and the Ch'i here is stimulated with plants, ensuring that visitors are instantly welcomed by a bright, fresh atmosphere. The major potential problem with this entrance is that a visitor may feel awkward if they enter the porch and come face to face with a closed hall door. To prevent this awkwardness, the hall door is panelled with glass and kept open during the day, making the whole place bright and inviting.

The turning staircase does create a dark corner at the top of the first flight. This can cause Ch'i energy to linger and stagnate and should be stimulated with a plant to keep the flow as smooth and beneficial as possible.

Since the hallway is in the north-eastern part of the house, the choice of blue for the carpeting is a good one.

If you are currently having financial difficulties, or are finding it difficult to handle the money which you do have, your bathroom may be playing a central role in these circumstances. Following the advice in this chapter will help you put a stop to such negative situations and begin to enjoy the flow of material wealth which has been eluding you.

THE DOOR

The door to the bathroom should open as wide as possible to allow an easy flow of Ch'i both in and out. The wider the door opens, the better, but unfortunately the opposite is also true. If your bathroom door does not open fully because there is a water fixture behind it (bath, shower, basin or toilet, for example), or because it opens against a wall, hang a mirror on both the outside and inside of the door to encourage a smoother and more productive flow of Ch'i.

ROOM SIZE

Traditionally the bathroom is one of the smallest rooms in the house. This may be all very well as far as architects and builders are concerned, but from a Feng Shui point of view nothing could be worse. If you consider your bathroom to be a kind of 'spiritual bank vault' then you will soon realise that the amount of prosperity you can experience is governed by the size of your bathroom. An extremely small bathroom creates an atmosphere of poverty and lack; an expansive bathroom creates a feeling of prosperity and opulence.

For this reason, no matter how large or small your bathroom is, you should aim to maximise it as fully as possible. This means you should have at least one large mirror in the bathroom to create the illusion of depth, and more than one mirror is preferable.

If the bathroom is narrower along one wall than the other, fix a large mirror to one of the longer walls. This will give the impression of widening the room and will allow more Ch'i to enter.

In extremely small bathrooms a mirror on the ceiling as well as the wall will give an excellent feeling of space and light, and can dramatically increase the wealth of your household. Many celebrities know this and cover the whole ceiling with one large mirror. Such a large mirror is not usually necessary, however, and even a small pane can bring excellent results.

Mirror tiles may be used sparingly, but only as a last resort. Because the reflected image they create is seldom uniform, the Ch'i surrounding the image may become equally distorted. Severe Ch'i distortion caused by mirror

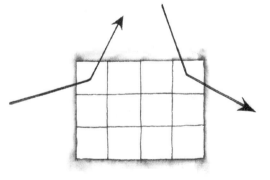

tiles can work against you, and instead of helping you achieve a greater level of material wealth and success, it may reduce the level you already have.

THE BATH / SHOWER

The bath or shower unit itself is the most important fixture in the bathroom. Ideally you should ensure that the unit is not beneath a window and that you have a full view of the door when bathing, but since this can only be arranged if you are fitting a suite for the first time (or are willing to move the existing suite and re-do the plumbing), you will probably have to use some of the following 'cures'.

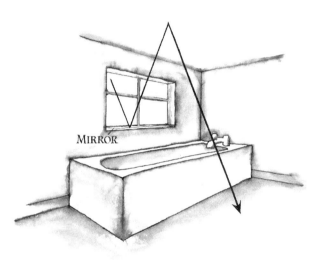

MIRROR

A bath which is positioned beneath the window poses a problem because, as the solar Ch'i enters the room in the form of natural light, the water in the bath will diffuse much of it before it has a chance to circulate through the whole of the bathroom. To solve this, fix a mirror to the window ledge so that incoming light is reflected up on to the ceiling and back down into the rest of the room.

A view of the door when bathing is important because, as you now know, being surprised by someone coming in unexpectedly will upset your bodily Ch'i quite badly. Again, if the bath is already fixed in a position where no clear view of the door is possible, use a mirror to give a reflected view.

The bath itself will normally be rectangular, and this is perfectly acceptable, but if you get the opportunity to install a circular or oval bath, take it! Circular and oval baths are very auspicious because they resemble the curves of a coin and this, in conjunction with the water within them, which symbolises money, helps to create a very good atmosphere of wealth and prosperity.

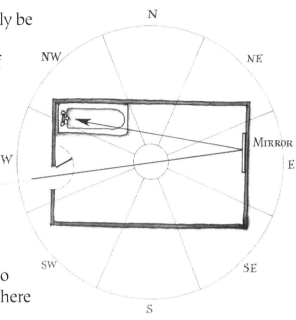

THE TOILET, BIDET AND BASIN

The section on page 164 discusses the ideal positioning of these items and the most effective Feng Shui solutions for a poorly placed toilet, bidet or basin. Beyond this, you should simply ensure that all items are uniform in colour. This will seldom be a problem because the most common suite colour is still white, but if you are in the rare position of having a basin, toilet or bidet which is a different colour to the rest of the suite, you should either replace it or paint it to match.

Starting from scratch

If you decide to install or move a bathroom suite, the most beneficial zones for the placement of items are as follows:

✳ The bath or shower unit should be placed to the north for spiritual wealth or to the south-east for material wealth. Do not place the bath or shower in the south because this is governed by the element of fire.

✳ The toilet should be placed in the north for spiritual wealth, or in any other zone except the south and south-east. The southern zone belongs to the element of fire, so if a toilet is placed in the south-east this could symbolise the 'flushing away' of money.

✳ A bidet or basin can be placed in any zone except the south. Once again, this is because the south belongs to the fire element.

If part of your bathroom suite is already positioned in the south and cannot be moved, place something black nearby. You could install black taps, fit a black hand rail or simply place a black ornament nearby. Because black belongs to the element of water, this will reduce any adverse effects of being in the fire zone. The bathroom will not make you feel very energetic if you do this, but at least your financial prosperity will remain intact.

If your toilet is currently situated in the south-east and cannot be moved, hang a purple ring on the wall. The purple colour will stimulate the wealth-creating energy of this zone and the ring symbolises the circulation of wealth, reminding you that what is flushed away is constantly re-entering your life in another, possibly even better form.

BATHROOM CHESTS AND CABINETS

These should be simple, functional items and, once again, fit in naturally with the colour scheme of your bathroom. Perhaps the most important thing to remember about bathroom chests and cabinets is that they should be used. This might sound like an odd thing to say, but from a Feng Shui perspective there is nothing worse than a bathroom cluttered with shampoo, conditioner and other bottles which are used on a regular basis. This is because the Ch'i of the room needs to flow as smoothly as possible, and a host of bottles, jars and other potions on view are not conducive to this flow.

If you haven't enough storage space to keep such items in the cabinet or chest you already have, you should either consider buying a larger unit or – the easiest solution – keep potions and lotions to a minimum. So many bathrooms are cluttered with bottles on display, yet few of them are used on a regular basis. Once the clutter is removed and the units used effectively, Ch'i flows better and the whole room will be more conducive to relaxation and clear thought.

DECOR

The bathroom should be decorated in whites or gently subtle colours. Avoid gaudy shades, except perhaps in small areas to bring out the energy of a particular zone. Co-ordinated suites, where the toilet, bath or shower unit and bidet are manufactured to a uniform design and colour, are best, but even plain white porcelains, enamels and metals are better than darker colours.

The floor of the bathroom should be tiled, but should not feel too cold as this will have a negative effect on the surrounding Ch'i energy. Special tiles are now available which cushion the feet and adapt to the temperature of the room, and these are ideal. Even better, they can be obtained in a wide variety of shades and this will help ensure that the whole of your bathroom is colour co-ordinated.

Use a blind instead of curtains and, of course, make sure it is waterproof so the steam in the room does not ruin the fabric.

LIGHT

Once again, the more natural light coming into the bathroom, the better. Most bathroom windows have frosted glass for the sake of privacy, but it is better to have plain glass unless you are overlooked. Plain glass does not diffuse the solar Ch'i anywhere near as much as frosted glass, and in this room especially you want as much energy as possible.

If you apply the principle of using mirrors, as we discussed earlier in this chapter, the bathroom will be one of the brightest rooms in the house. This will make it more Yang than Yin and you will find that after bathing you feel charged with energy and vitality.

Lamps and other electrical items are not recommended for use in the bathroom because this would increase the risk of accidents. A professionally fitted ceiling light or wall light is usually sufficient; if further light is required floating candles can stimulate the Ch'i of the room quite dramatically.

SOUND

The sound of running water is all that is needed to stimulate the energy in this room, but hanging a wind chime in any zone will help stimulate that area. Hanging a chime in the north, which itself belongs to the element of water, will promote greater spiritual experience and career progression.

A chime in the eastern zone will promote a greater level of personal contentment and optimism for the future. Chimes should not be hung in the south because you really do not want to stimulate the fire zone in a room which is primarily water-orientated.

Playing soft instrumental music whilst bathing in the evening will help you relax, but if you bathe or shower in the morning play up-tempo music which will stimulate the Ch'i of the room more dramatically and charge you with Yang. This will give you plenty of energy and set you up for a very productive day.

LIFE (LIVING THINGS)

Plants are the best form of life to introduce to the bathroom, but make your selection carefully. Bathrooms are typically warm rooms and the air has a high moisture content, so plants which thrive in this type of atmosphere are obviously better than those which are better suited to a dry environment.

Place plants in zones where you want to stimulate the associated Ch'i energy. If you want to improve your sense of self-motivation and knowledge, a plant placed in the north-east will help you accomplish this. If a greater sense of optimism about life is your goal, a plant in the east would be more suitable.

COLOUR

Bringing out the specific energies of certain zones is not difficult in the bathroom because there are always a variety of small coloured items which you can place around the room without imposing too much on the overall decor. Towel racks, toothbrush holders and other similar items will blend in quite naturally with the bathroom, even if they are strongly coloured.

For example, a purple towel rack in the south-east will stimulate the wealth and creativity section of the room; a pink toilet-roll holder or toothbrush holder will improve the quality of your relationships and increase the amount of tranquillity you experience within them.

If porcelain tiles are used to decorate the bathroom (as opposed to mirrored tiles which, as I said earlier, are not recommended), you could activate the Ch'i in a zone by having one coloured tile among

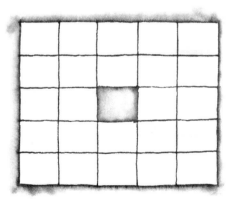

the others. For example, if you want to activate the north-western energy zone to help you improve your planning and leadership abilities, you could have a single grey tile set among a wall of white tiles. This will not look out of place, but rather will give each zone its own 'personality'.

To sum up ...

Improving the flow of Ch'i in your bathroom according to the principles we have discussed in this chapter will help totally revolutionise your financial life. Money will flow into your home as never before, and material difficulties will soon be a thing of the past.

IMPROVE YOUR LIFESTYLE

How Feng Shui can help you cope with some common problems

Question

Bathtime for me is for total relaxation: forgetting all my worries and luxuriating! So I want the bathroom to be as relaxing as possible. How can Feng Shui help?

Answer

Placing a cassette player in the northern zone and using it to play soothing music whilst bathing will stimulate the Ch'i associated with tranquillity with both sound and electricity – even if the player is battery operated. Use this in conjunction with the more general principles outlined in this chapter and your bathtime will become a haven of peace and restoration.

Question

I use my time lying in the bath as 'thinking time': trying to work out problems, sort out the family finances, etc. Can Feng Shui help me clear my mind and find a way through the problems to a solution?

Answer

The zone which needs stimulating in this case is that of the north-west, because this area governs leadership, planning and responsibility of all kinds. Placing one or two crystals on a small metal tray will work wonders because both the crystals and the metal will stimulate the surrounding Ch'i. The result should be a noticeable increase in your clarity of thought.

Question

I often read in the bath, both 'trashy' novels for relaxation and work reports. Can Feng Shui help create an atmosphere which is conducive to both?

Answer

The zone to stimulate here is the south-west, since this governs both tranquillity and practicality, thus helping you to be both relaxed enough to enjoy your novels and practical enough to retain the information in work reports.

To stimulate the south-west, consider placing a small vase of artificial pink flowers in this area. Artificial flowers are easier to maintain than real ones, especially in a bathroom setting. Nevertheless, both the colour pink and the representation of life will stimulate the surrounding Ch'i quite well, helping you to achieve your two-fold aim easily and effectively.

Question

Our bathroom has to cater for adults, adolescents and an elderly grandparent, all with conflicting needs and differing ideas of what bathrooms are for and how long you need to stay in them...! Can Feng Shui deal with these differing needs?

Answer

To ensure that the bathroom is suitable for all, you should try to stick to the general Feng Shui principles which I outlined earlier in this chapter. Specific zones should not deliberately be stimulated unless everyone who uses the bathroom on a regular basis is striving to achieve the same things in life. Having said that, placing one crystal on a small metal or white tray in the western zone will ensure that everyone who uses the bathroom will become more considerate of others. This should help reduce any stress which bathtimes currently cause.

Question

I share a bathroom with three students/work colleagues/ housemates and we all seem to descend on it at once. Can Feng Shui help create a more sharing atmosphere, one more conducive to considering the needs of others?

Answer

Again, it is the western zone which needs stimulating here, so apply the same solution offered for the last question. You should also discuss your bathroom arrangements when you and your housemates are relaxed and comfortable, such as over dinner. Chances are that they are just as frustrated as you, and will be keen to resolve the situation to the benefit of all concerned.

8

HALLWAYS

At the beginning of this book I explained how bodily Ch'i flows along something called meridians and is stored in seven energy centres called chakras. In your home the rooms can be likened to these chakras and hallways act as the meridians, allowing the Ch'i energy to flow back and forth between rooms.

If Ch'i is to flow smoothly and effectively throughout your home your hallways should be as free of obstructions as possible and the Ch'i should flow steadily along them. Ch'i which flows too fast down hallways can make everyone in your household feel pressured and this can lead to nervous disorders and tension. Ch'i which moves too slowly along hallways can have the opposite effect in the long term, making residents feel tired, apathetic and prone to extreme procrastination.

The speed at which Ch'i flows along a hallway depends on the size and shape of the hallway itself, and in this chapter we will look at

▶ STUDY

The desk in this home office is situated in the south-eastern zone, which is perfect for increasing levels of wealth and creativity. However, the desk faces the wall, which can make the user feel a little claustrophobic. In addition, the user has no clear view of the door when seated. To solve both of these problems, the desk should be moved so that the user has his back to the wall when seated.

The large open bookcase is a likely source of negative Ch'i daggers, but these are not fired directly towards the desk, so no great harm will be caused. Just to be safe, however, a small crystal should be placed on each shelf to help keep the flow of Ch'i in these regions as user-friendly as possible.

▶ OFFICE IN A CONSERVATORY

This is an extremely good example of a room built as a conservatory which has been converted to another use, in this case a home office. Note how much natural light the room receives, but how the clever use of blinds enables the user to work in privacy at the same time.

The main problems in this room are the positioning of the desk and the open bookcases. The desk at present does not allow a clear view of the door, but if a mirror were positioned where the noticeboard is currently situated, a reflected view would be provided without the user having to sacrifice his wonderful garden view.

The open bookcases, situated immediately next to and behind the office chair, will undoubtedly cause some problems. They should either be replaced with bookcases which have doors or moved to another part of the office altogether.

Finally, the plants in this room give the Ch'i a constant source of stimulation and help it to flow as smoothly as possible. What's more, because this room was originally built as a conservatory, the plants will thrive with a minimum of attention.

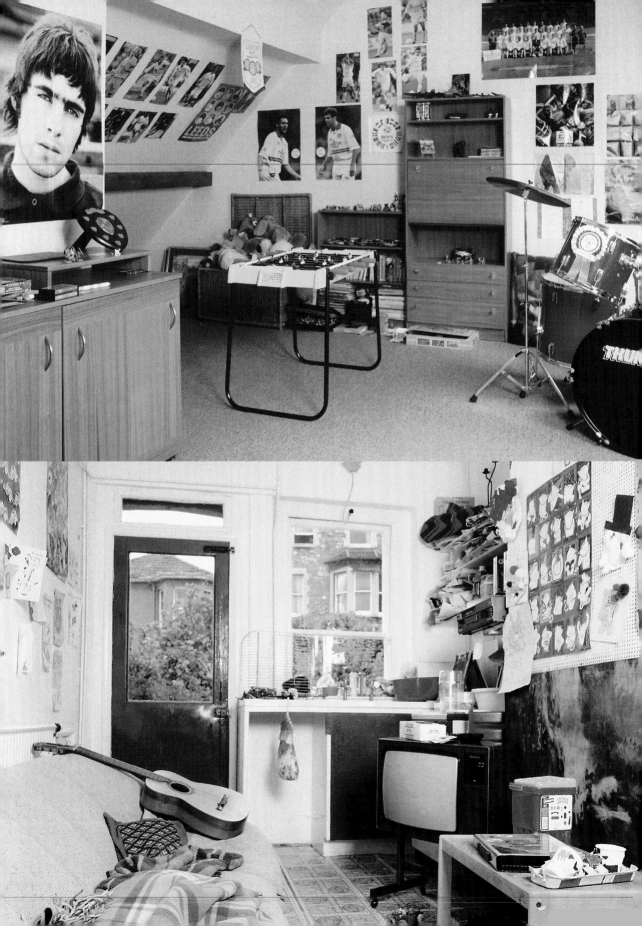

◄ CHILDREN'S PLAYROOM

Here a loft has been converted into a playroom for youngsters, and to ensure that the room is as well lit as possible, ceiling lights have been set into opposing angles. Lights would also be useful in the corners of the room, because these would help to stimulate any slow-moving Ch'i which gathers there.

The relatively plain decor is made more vibrant with colourful posters which appeal to the children who use the room on a regular basis, and when the occupants decide to play the drums it is certain that all Ch'i energy in the room will be stimulated quite strongly!

If any one thing requires attention it is the collection of toys in the open toy chest. The chest should be closed when not in use, so some of the excess toys should be moved to another location or placed on top of the closed chest in an orderly fashion. As far as children's playrooms go, however, this is a good example of what can be achieved in even the most unconventional of places.

◄ FAMILY ROOM

This long, narrow family room has been converted from a utility room. It is surprisingly well lit, thanks to the plain glass in the door next to the window. A greater illusion of space, however, could be achieved by placing a large mirror opposite the sofa. This would also give occupants a reflected view of the door when seated.

The worst aspect of this room is the clutter to the right of the window, with shelves bursting at the seams. This is not good from a Feng Shui point of view, and there really is no need for it. Look closely under the window and you will see that there is a precious amount of unused space here in which a cupboard could be positioned. This would remove the clutter from the shelves and allow the Ch'i of the room to flow much more smoothly.

ways of helping ensure smooth and consistent energy flow. This will make the Ch'i of the rooms in your home even more balanced and so benefit every area of your life, from family relationships and success, to the quality of your sex life and financial prosperity.

NARROW HALLS WITH NO DOORS OR WINDOWS

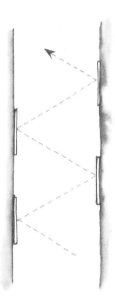

Narrow halls which have no doors or windows to either side leave the Ch'i energy no option but to travel quickly from one end to the other. This means that the energy travels faster than is desirable, so we must find some way of slowing it down.

The most common method of slowing down Ch'i in a narrow hall of this type is to hang mirrors or pictures behind glass on either side of the hall in such a way that the energy 'zig-zags' its way from one side to the other as it travels along. Ch'i reflects off the mirror or glass. This will naturally slow down the flow of energy to a more desirable level.

Another method is to use plants. Place plants on either side of the hallway, in an arrangement similar to the one shown for mirrors. This will create 'obstacles' which slow down the Ch'i, but will also stimulate the energy beneficially.

NARROW HALLS WITH DOORS OR WINDOWS

If a narrow hall does have one or more doors or windows along its length, slowing down Ch'i is even easier. All you need to do is open a door or window a few inches so that the Ch'i has somewhere to go rather than flowing simply from one end of the hall to the other.

WIDE HALLS

In wide halls, Ch'i moves slowly. In a wide hall which has many doors or windows the majority should be closed, otherwise the Ch'i flow will become even slower. Even when this has been done, Ch'i will not be flowing as smoothly as we would like, so further corrective measures must be taken.

One common way of increasing the speed of the flow is to hang small crystals in a straight line at intervals from one end of the hall to another. This gives the Ch'i a natural 'flight path' and will discourage excessive straying, improving the flow quite considerably.

DECOR

Because the Ch'i flowing through a hallway is travelling from room to room, the hallway itself should be as neutral as possible. This means there should be a balance between Yin and Yang, with no particular zones in a hallway deliberately stimulated. From an interior design point of view this makes hallways the easiest sections of a home to deal with, since good Feng Shui here is simply a matter of creating a sense of balance.

Aim to use angles and curves and hard and soft furnishings in roughly equal proportions, so that Yin and Yang are similarly balanced. For example, if there is a lot of wood in the hall (such as an expansive wooden floor), counter this by hanging soft, gentle curtains. Similarly, if the hall is structurally very curved, consider balancing this by hanging a few large rectangular or square paintings.

Plants shouldn't be used unless the hall is narrow, according to earlier instructions. Furniture should also be avoided because halls, according to Feng Shui, should be as uncluttered as possible.

LIGHT

Here again, balance is the key. Natural light should be encouraged as much as possible because solar Ch'i is almost always beneficial, but avoid using strong artificial lights such as fluorescent strip lights, since these are extremely Yang and will affect the energy which flows past them. Wall lights staggered along either side of a hallway are usually the best option for evening illumination, as they both provide light and at the same time cast shadows, presenting an ideal balance between Yin and Yang.

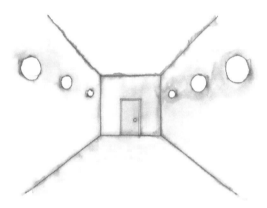

To sum up ...

Because we want the hallways to be smooth meridians along which the Ch'i energy of your home can flow in a consistent and uniform manner, there is seldom any reason to introduce elements of sound, movement or specific colour to these areas. Once you have slowed down or increased the speed of the Ch'i according to how wide your hallway is and have balanced Yin and Yang through decor and lighting, nothing further is to be done. Simply ensure that the hallways are kept free of unwanted obstructions as far as possible and relax in the knowledge that the meridians of your home are serving their purpose well.

IMPROVE YOUR LIFESTYLE

How Feng Shui can help you cope with some common problems

Question

I want to make the entrance hall of my home a welcoming area. What should I do?

Answer

The best way to make guests feel instantly welcome is to hang a mobile or crystal from the centre of the hall ceiling. This will stimulate the central zone, increasing the health of everyone passing through, but it will also stimulate the other eight zones, thus improving their wealth, energy, relationships, and so on. You should also ensure that the hall does not feel cramped or crowded. If it does and there is nothing you can do to create more space in the hall itself, you should hang a large mirror or two on the walls of the hall to give the illusion of space. Last, but by no means least, you should stimulate the bodily energy of your guests by being careful to greet them with a smile.

Question

We would like our entrance hall to be an attractive place. What could we put there that would have beneficial Feng Shui effects?

Answer

Mirrors are always beneficial, and ornate mirrors give a decorative quality which instantly increase the attractiveness of a hall. The decor should not be too dark, as this will cause the energy of the hall to lean too heavily towards Yin. Instead aim for a bright, airy feel. Large items of furniture should be avoided as much as possible but a small table with a vase or two of fresh flowers almost always improves the impression a hall gives. The life of the plants will also help to stimulate the surrounding Ch'i. As long as you work to the rule 'the simpler and brighter the better', you can be confident that your hall will be as attractive as it can be.

Question

I don't want the hallways in my home just to be areas people pass through on their way to other rooms which are seen as more important; I would like the hallways to provide a breathing space within the house. How can I use Feng Shui to give them their own character and beauty?

Answer

Just as mirrors and plants can be used to slow down the movement of Ch'i from one end of the hall to another, so certain items can be similarily placed to encourage people to enjoy the room for its own sake. The most simple items are usually the most effective – both from a Feng Shui and decorative point of view. Framed portraits of family members hung on either side of the hall (or diagonally up a staircase wall) give guests something to experience as they make their way from A to B.

If your hall has certain features which often go unnoticed, such as particularly decorative carpentry work, you can attract attention to these areas by highlighting them with a small vase of flowers or decorative crystal. This will stimulate the surrounding Ch'i and encourage guests to enjoy the feature fully before continuing.

If no particular feature is present and you feel that you simply must place an item of furniture in a hall, consider obtaining a trophy or crystal case to hang on the largest wall. This can then be used to display a tasteful selection of ornaments, trophies or other items which you think will be of interest.

Question

We have to use some of the space in the hallway (under the stairs) for storage of school bags, musical instruments, etc. How can we mitigate the bad Ch'i effects of this unavoidable clutter?

Answer

As you rightly imply, some amount of clutter is unavoidable in all homes. Some cupboards, such as ones below stairs, are particularly likely to be used as general storage areas, and if left untended can disrupt the smooth flow of Ch'i quite considerably. Fortunately, the solution in these cases is very simple. Hang or place a small crystal inside the cupboard to disperse negative Ch'i and smooth what would otherwise be a very unnatural flow of energy.

9

OTHER ROOMS

I n this chapter we will take a look at seven other rooms which your home might have: a conservatory, a home office, a children's play-room, a nursery, a study, a workroom and a studio. I will make suggestions as to whether these rooms should be Yin or Yang and where you might want to position particular pieces of furniture to experience more wealth, success, and so on. The general principles we have used in previous chapters can also be used in any of these rooms, of course.

THE CONSERVATORY

A conservatory is classically defined as 'a greenhouse for exotics', meaning that it is primarily a room which is dedicated to the propagation of plant life. Today, however, a conservatory is seen as something much more. It is a quiet place where you can sit and relax in close proximity to plant life and develop the intuitive, spiritual side of your nature.

Because tranquillity and spirituality are important to most people who have a conservatory, the best place for such a room is on the northern side of the house. This may not necessarily be the best position for plants as far as sunlight is concerned, however, and that is why you must decide what you really want from a conservatory before you have one built, or organise one.

If you have yet to build a conservatory decide exactly what you expect to gain from having such a room. If you want to experience a deeper sense of your spiritual awareness, the north of the building is an ideal site. If, on the other hand, you want to tap into your creative abilities and write a novel in your conservatory, the area to the south-east of the building would be more appropriate.

The ideal shape of your conservatory also depends on what you intend to get out of it. If you intend to relax in your conservatory, a curved Yin shape such as a circle or oval would be more fitting than a predominantly Yang shape such as a square or rectangle. The latter two shapes would be more suitable if you intend to do something active in the room, such as exercise or play games.

Generally speaking, however, conservatories are intended to be relaxing, so the energy of the room should lean further towards Yin than Yang. Natural light will, of course, feature heavily in the room, but when artificial lighting is called for, use standard or wall lamps to give a warm, pleasing glow, rather than, for example, Yang-creating spotlights.

The layout of a conservatory is largely a matter of personal preference. Many people place chairs or other seats in the centre of the room, but since this is the central zone as far as Feng Shui is concerned, it should be left as unobstructed as possible.

Seating should therefore be placed towards the edge of a conservatory. If spirituality and tranquillity are important to you, sitting in the northern zone of the room would be most beneficial. If, on the other hand, you would like your conservatory to help you develop your creativity, sitting in the south-eastern zone would be more appropriate.

Plants, of course, usually feature quite heavily in a conservatory and these can be scattered around the room to stimulate every zone at the same time. With so much life (living things) in a conservatory you can expect to feel refreshed and energised even after spending just a short time sitting in the room, and in the long term your quality and appreciation of life will improve dramatically.

THE HOME OFFICE

The number of people who work from home is increasing at an astonishing rate. Working from home solves problems associated with commuting through heavy traffic and is now widely accepted as a more enlightened way of operating.

If you have a home office you can improve your work and productivity quite markedly by applying the principles of Feng Shui to the room. Ideally a home office would lie towards the south-east, north-west, north or north-east of the building, since these areas respectively govern wealth, responsibility, career and motivation.

Because a home office is primarily a place in which you want to get things done, the energy within it should be more Yang than Yin. This means that you should give preference to angles over curves and decorate to give as much sense of light as possible. Blinds should be used instead of curtains to allow a maximum flow of solar Ch'i into the room, and bright spotlights used for any evening work.

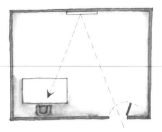

The main item of furniture in any home office is the desk. This should be positioned so that you have a full view of the door when seated; if this is not possible, a mirror should be hung to provide a reflected view.

Ideally the desk should never face a wall because this will slow down the flow of your bodily Ch'i, and in the long term will make you feel claustrophobic and trapped. If you must face the wall because of lack of space, however, then either sit in front of a window or hang a picture of a far-away landscape above your desk to give the wall some feeling of depth and reduce any 'closed-in' feelings you might otherwise experience.

Most home work involves the storage of files or books. To avoid suffering from negative 'Ch'i-daggers' ensure that such items are not in your direct line of sight. Instead, consider investing in bookshelves or filing cabinets which have doors. This will allow circulating Ch'i to flow smoothly over the surface of the doors.

WRONG

RIGHT

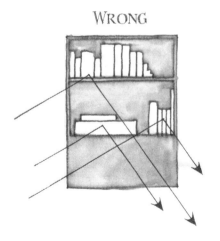

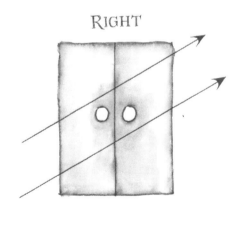

THE PLAYROOM

A playroom which is specifically used by children should ideally be situated in the eastern, south-eastern or northern part of the building, because these areas respectively govern contentment, creativity and tranquillity. The room should have a balance between Yin and Yang because a leaning in either direction could cause apathy or hyperactivity.

Once again, natural light is to be encouraged as much as possible, but if the room is to be used in the evenings then a central ceiling light with a yellow shade (to stimulate the yellow health energy of the central zone) would be best. Standard and other free-standing lamps should be avoided in a playroom because of the danger which they may present to small children, although this is obviously less of a problem the older your children are.

There are few standard items in a playroom because the taste of children is constantly changing. Here are some fairly typical items found in a playroom, however, and the best positions for them:

✳ Sand pits should be positioned in the north-eastern or south-western zones because sand is closely linked with the earth element of these zones. If you want to bring out the qualities associated with these areas (motivation and tranquillity respectively) then use a blue sand pit in the north-east or a pink one in the south-west.

✳ Water tanks designed for children to play with should be positioned in the northern zone because this belongs to the water element. A black tank will bring out the tranquillity of this zone, but if you think that's a bit too gloomy, try using a more brightly coloured tank and painting black dots on it. This will still stimulate the energy of the zone but will look a lot more fun.

✳ Wooden toys should be positioned in the eastern or south-eastern zone because both of these areas belong to the element of wood. A green poster in the east will make your children feel more contented; a purple poster in the south-east will make them feel more creative.

Despite your best intentions to keep toys in their 'ideal' Feng Shui positions, children will not quite see the relevance of this and naturally things will tend to get scattered about the room. Go with the flow! The children's freedom is just as important as good Feng Shui, and as long as they are happy and contented while they play, they will not suffer any negative effects.

THE NURSERY

Because the nursery is primarily a room where babies and very young children sleep, the best position for this room is in the northern section of the house. This is because the north governs tranquillity and is most conducive to sleep and relaxation. Yin should be slightly more dominant than Yang during the day so that the occupiers do not become restless. To achieve this, avoid excessive artificial lighting and concentrate instead on using night lights which illuminate the room but are not so bright as to keep your baby or young child awake.

✳ The cot or bed should be positioned in the northern zone and the area kept free of clutter. Do not allow the sleeping area to contain too many toys as this will obstruct the flow of Ch'i in the room, which needs to be as smooth as possible. You should also be careful to avoid stimulating the southern zone, which can cause restlessness and broken sleep.

✳ If a baby monitor is used so that you can hear your child in another room if he or she wakes, the best position for this is in the eastern zone, since the electrical current running through the monitor will stimulate the Ch'i associated with health and contentment.

✳ Baby changing units and other items of furniture should be rounded rather than angled and positioned for convenience. As long as the southern zone is not stimulated through the colour red or an electrical current, the previous steps taken will ensure a good night's sleep for your child.

THE STUDY

A study is most commonly a place of academic work or work associated with leisure pursuits and hobbies. Because of this, the best position for a study is in the north-eastern part of the building, which governs the expansion of knowledge.

Yin and Yang should be roughly balanced, so make sure that the whole of the room is evenly lit. Natural light is obviously preferable to artificial, but when the latter does have to be used, standard lamps are usually the most effective in giving good study conditions without flooding the room with a lot of Yang energy.

As you would expect, the best position for seating in this room is in the north-eastern zone. Again, this is because this zone is best suited to learning and the development of knowledge. The seating should be positioned so the occupier has a full view of the door. If this is not possible, then a mirror or two should be hung so that a reflected view of the door is given.

Finally, you should follow the advice given in the 'home office' section of this chapter (see page 187) as far as the storage of books is concerned. This is particularly important in a study where there are a lot of books, since Ch'i can, as I said earlier, be disrupted quite badly by the open storage of books; the more there are, the greater the potential disruption.

THE WORKROOM

A workroom is normally used for ironing, sewing and carrying out other household tasks, so it is important that the room is conducive to practicality but is also relaxing for the occupant. Since the south-western zone governs both tranquillity and practicality, having a workroom in the south-west of a house will be most beneficial from a Feng Shui perspective.

Yang should dominate in a workroom so that the occupier will find it easier to get things done. Bright light should therefore be encouraged and dark corners made to appear lighter and more spacious by hanging mirrors in them.

The items of furniture you use in your workroom will depend primarily on the type of work you do on a regular basis. Generally speaking, a workroom will contain ironing, sewing and perhaps even DIY facilities, but this list is by no means exhaustive. The three 'rules of thumb' to apply to a workroom are:

✳ Try and make sure that you use the south-western zone of the room as much as possible. This will make you more relaxed when tackling practical jobs.

✳ Keep the workroom tidy and organised. Clutter in the workroom – as in all other rooms – disrupts the flow of energy, and this is never beneficial.

✳ If the weather permits, open a window while you are working so that more solar Ch'i can enter the room. This will charge you with Yang energy and prevent you from feeling too tired when tackling long or repetitive chores.

THE STUDIO

A studio which is used primarily for painting, drawing and other creative endeavours, is ideally sited in the south-eastern zone which governs all forms of creativity. Yang should dominate so that you feel active and vibrant when working in this room, so this means that the studio should be as bright as possible. Painting the walls white and ensuring that as much natural light as possible enters through the windows will go a long way to achieving this goal.

Your primary workplace should be situated in the south-eastern part of the studio. Not only will this ensure that you are always at your best as far as creativity is concerned, but since this is also the zone which governs wealth, your work is likely to help you improve your financial status too.

Having a full view of the door is particularly important in a creative atmosphere, because being unexpectedly disturbed can radically disrupt the flow of Ch'i in the room and make it difficult to return to a smooth channel of creative expression. For this reason, make sure that you can always see the door whilst working, either directly or with the help of strategically hung mirrors.

Many artists allow their studios to become cluttered with previous works which they have completed or which are in development; this is bad for the flow of Ch'i and should be avoided at all costs. If possible, consider installing a large cupboard in which work can be stored. An alternative, but perhaps rather less convenient arrangement, is to store work in a separate room.

To sum up ...

As discussed earlier, all Feng Shui principles can be applied to these rooms just as to a bedroom, kitchen etc. Introduce plants, crystals, chimes, mobiles and other items into the rooms for specific Ch'i stimulation according to the following chart, which you are now very familiar with.

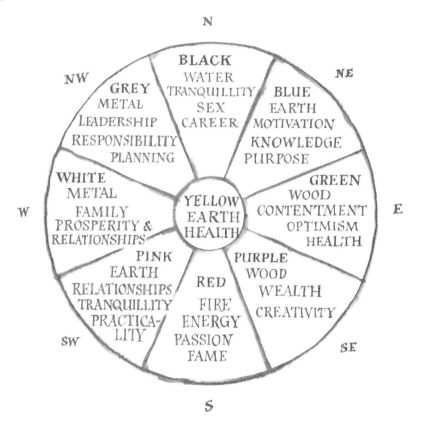

IMPROVE YOUR LIFESTYLE

How Feng Shui can help you cope with some common problems

CONSERVATORY
Question

We use the conservatory as a family room for all sorts of purposes: to relax, read, keep plants, sew, paint, draw, listen to music, prepare work, study documents, do homework, etc. Can Feng Shui principles cater for such a general purpose room, and help make it conducive to both work and play?

Answer

If such a wide variety of activities are to take place in the conservatory, the best thing to do from a Feng Shui point of view is to stimulate the central zone. Hanging a plant, mobile or wind chime in the centre of the conservatory will stimulate the energy of the central zone (which governs general health), but will also stimulate – albeit to a lesser extent – the energy of the other eight directions.

By taking this approach the conservatory will be conducive to all kinds of activities, be they work or relaxation. As a result the whole family will be able to benefit from being in this room, even if different activities take place simultaneously.

Question

I keep my exercise bike in the conservatory, so I want to promote an energetic atmosphere. What should I do?

Answer

You have a choice between stimulating the southern zone which governs energy, or the eastern zone which governs health. Since I assume you are using your exercise bike to develop and/or maintain a general state of good health, I suggest that your exercise bike is positioned in the eastern zone. Stimulate the Ch'i of this direction by placing a green plant in that area, and if you really want to experience a higher level of energy, activate the southern Ch'i by placing a red object in that part of the conservatory.

Naturally, Yang should predominate because this is most conducive to activity, but this will be automatic as long as your conservatory receives plenty of light. If you exercise in the evening, use bright lights instead of dim ones. Regardless of the time of day, having a cassette player or radio playing up-beat music in the eastern zone will stimulate the energy of health even more through a combination of sound and electricity.

HOME OFFICE
Question

I work from home and find it hard to get started in the morning. I want to create a room which will feel different from the rest of the house, will promote efficiency, hard work, productivity and professionalism, and get me into 'work mode' easily and quickly. Help, please!

Answer

The ideal workplace is one where Yang dominates, so the first thing you must do is ensure that your home office receives as much natural light as possible. This is best achieved by using blinds instead of curtains and hanging a mirror next to the window to attract more light into the room. That done, you should arrange your office so that your desk is in the north-western, northern or south-eastern zone. The north-western zone governs leadership, responsibility and planning; the northern zone your general career, and the south-eastern zone creativity and wealth. You should select the zone to work in according to which of these qualities you feel is most important to your business.

Once you have positioned your desk, you should stimulate the other two zones through the placement of plants, crystals or objects which correspond to the colour and/or element of those zones. For example, if you place your desk in the northern career zone, you might stimulate the energies of the other two zones by placing a grey metal filing cabinet in the north-west and a purple picture with a wooden frame in the south-east.

By working in one specific zone and stimulating the other two, you will have the best possible Feng Shui set-up for a productive and satisfying home office.

PLAYROOM
Question

How can Feng Shui help us create a happy, healthy and fun play area for the children, while minimising their arguments? Suggestions, please.

Answer

The best solution here is to stimulate the Ch'i of both the east and the south-east, since these zones respectively govern contentment and creativity. Stimulation of these zones can be accomplished if wooden toys are placed in these areas. Try to add an element of green in the east and of purple in the south-east for even better stimulation.

Since many arguments between young children often stem from boredom (lack of creativity) or jealousy (a lack of contentment), taking this approach should reduce their frequency quite dramatically. This will allow your children to spend more time playing peacefully and develop into healthy, balanced individuals.

NURSERY
Question

My baby is a poor sleeper. He/she doesn't settle easily and often wakes during the night. Can I use Feng Shui to encourage him/her to settle and sleep well?

Answer

If possible, place the cot or bed in the northern zone. This zone governs tranquillity and is normally the best for helping to solve sleeping difficulties. Stimulating the Ch'i of this zone by introducing a black cuddly toy or teething ring, etc., will bring noticeable benefits. One thing you must avoid, however, is an excess of the colour red, since this colour is associated with the fire element and may cause restlessness.

STUDY
Question

I want to use Feng Shui to create the best possible environment for my academic studies/job-related work/committee/work. Suggestions please.

Answer

You should try to stimulate the energy in both the north-west and north-east. The north-west governs leadership, responsibility and planning, and stimulating this zone will help you set about your studies and work in a productive, organised manner. Similarly, stimulation of the north-east will increase your ability to concentrate and retain information. You should stimulate both of these zones with large plants, as these will also help to keep the atmosphere fresh and invigorating.

WORKROOM
Question

I use this room for sewing or ironing (to music!), where I can get on with essential household work and enjoy some peace and quiet away from the family hubbub. It needs to have a productive yet relaxing atmosphere. How can Feng Shui help?

Answer

Stimulating the south-western zone will work wonders. Place a pink-flowered pot plant in this zone and the Ch'i energy will be stimulated by the plant itself, the soil the plant is bedded in and the colour pink. Since this zone governs both tranquillity and practicality, the activated Ch'i in this area will help you to perform practical household tasks with a great deal of ease – and remain relaxed at the same time.

STUDIO
Question

I use this room for professional/amateur painting/drawing/ illustration. The atmosphere needs to be peaceful, but creative and receptive to ideas. What Feng Shui principles should I employ?

Answer

Stimulate the northern zone by placing a small aquarium or black bowl of fresh water in this area. This will provide the element of peace you are looking for, but you must be sure to change the water on a daily basis, because if it is anything less than fresh the amount of tranquillity you experience in this room will plummet. Once that is done, aim to work in the south-eastern zone. If possible, work at a wooden easel, as wood is associated with the creative Ch'i of this zone. Another thing which some artists have found beneficial is to tie a purple ribbon on their easel. This will encourage even more creativity, especially in the immediate working vicinity.

CONCLUSION
The Ideal
Feng Shui Home

As I have shown in this book, Feng Shui is not a collection of rigid rules which are to be followed to the letter. Rather, it is an art applied through the lens of your own personality and tastes, so there really is no such thing as an 'ideal' Feng Shui home.

What is ideal for you in Feng Shui terms may not work for another person, and vice versa. By applying the principles of Feng Shui in your own style, however, your home can truly be ideal for you and your family and have dramatic effects on the whole of your life.

By applying the principles of Feng Shui to your home in the way I have described, you and your family will experience life on a whole new level. Instead of fighting with the universe in order to get what you want, much of what you desire will come automatically because you are now operating *with* spiritual law instead of against it:

✳ Your lounge will become the room in which family relationships are forged and nurtured;

✳ Your kitchen will become the room from which health and financial well-being will flourish;

✳ Your dining room will be the room where you strengthen social and business relationships;

✳ Your bedroom will be a place of spiritual tranquillity, rejuvenation and sexual satisfaction;

✳ Your bathroom will unlock a flow of wealth into your life;

✳ Even your hallways will help the Ch'i of the universe fill your life with its blessings!

And this leads me back to where I began this book ...

What leads many people to set aside today's complex technologies and focus instead on the simple practices of a metaphysical art which is older than Christianity? Why is Feng Shui as popular today in the Western world as it has been in the East for many centuries?

The only possible explanation, and one which many thousands of people will testify to, is that Feng Shui gets results.

I hope that, by following the simple principles I have revealed in this book, you come to experience these life-enhancing results for yourself.

TEMPLATE

Use photocopies of this page to draw up your room plans. Make a rough sketch first and establish the direction and measurements before you make your final drawings.

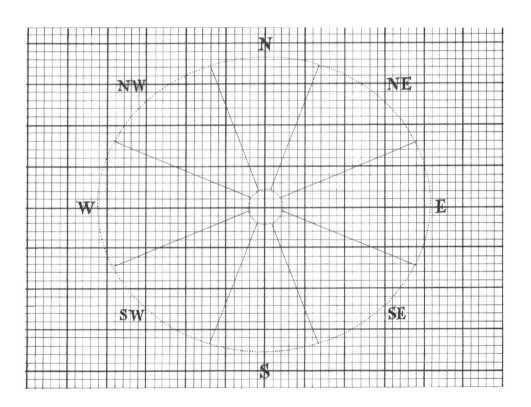

INDEX OF

COMMON PROBLEMS

INDEX